PRAISE FOR *Mary Jo Pehl* AND

EMPLOYEE OF THE MONTH

"This book marks the end of Mary Jo Pehl's secret reign as one of America's funniest women. Now everyone will know."
—Alonso Duralde, Author of *101 Must-See Movies for Gay Men*

"So hilarious is EMPLOYEE OF THE MONTH that it has just received the prestigious 'Joel Hodgson Award' for general funniness in book form!"
—Joel Hodgson, Creator, *Mystery Science Theater 3000*
and *Cinematic Titanic*

"There was this one time I made pork chops and served them to Mary Jo Pehl and they were the toughest, driest, least flavorful pork chops that had ever been created. But she ate her entire chop and told me it was delicious. That means she's a liar. And liars are the best people because they make great storytellers, which is another thing she is."
—Dave White, Author of *Exile in Guyville*

"Mary Jo describes herself as 'compulsively truthful,' and that pathological honesty (about herself and others) shines through in this deeply funny collection of tales. Few people have such a finely-tuned radar for the absurdities of life."

—J. Elvis Weinstein, Writer/Producer, *Cinematic Titanic*
and *Freaks and Geeks*

"In these essays, Mary Jo Pehl invites you into her carefully-observed, slightly skewed and most of all, funny world. It's a world you'll be glad you entered."

—Lorna Landvik, Author of *Angry Housewives Eating Bon Bons*

"If this book is even 1/10th as wonderful as the woman that is Mary Jo Pehl you will be so overcome that you will purchase this book every time you see it.

Damn."

—Smoove B., Columnist for *The Onion*

"Mary Jo Pehl can do what very few authors can—make me laugh out loud. Like an anthropologist, she has collected these hilarious and honest tales of travel, romantic encounters, and moving stories of, well... moving. She presents this fieldwork here in a 'cabinet of wonders' for us to open and enjoy."

—Trace Beaulieu

EMPLOYEE OF THE MONTH

EMPLOYEE OF THE MONTH
and Other Big Deals

MARY JO PEHL

Illustrations by Len Peralta

For THR
Until August 31ˢᵗ

Introduction:
A Do-Over

So it's like this: several years ago, a very small publishing company approached me about writing a book. Now, just about everyone wants to write a book, and no one more so than a *writer*. My goodness, I'd been putting pen to paper ever since I read *Harriet the Spy* in elementary school, and like the heroine, I began carrying notebooks and jotting notes about everything. I'm not really sure why *Harriet the Spy* had that effect. I'd read *Les Miserables* and never stole a loaf of bread (Wonder Bread was plentiful in our house, so maybe I realized how senseless it would be).

But, oh, how I was *a writer!* I used a fountain pen, I tortured metaphors like I'd been trained at the School of the Americas, and I had a profound grasp of Cat Stevens' lyrics. Here is a passage from my junior-high journal, copied *verbatim* from the worn, college-ruled yellow notebook.

> *People are like taco chips. Some have all the spice and*
> *powdery stuff, and yet others have very little. But they are*
> *all consumed for their individual worth.*

You will probably need a few minutes to reflect on that. Then there was the period when I was an impassioned, keening, garment-rending and breast-beating (mine, not someone else's) fan of the Minnesota Vikings.

> *February 4, 1975*
> *I feel like nobody cares about anything anymore. It's been*
> *this way since the Minnesota Vikings lost to Dallas in the*
> *playoffs, and no one seems as upset as I do. Maybe I should*
> *see a psychiatrist or something. Dallas shouldn't have won.*
> *It was a game of miscalls. It's ironic though—the very day*
> *that Dallas beat the Minnesota Vikings, Fran Tarkenton's*
> *father died—whose name was Dallas.*

The point is, dear reader, if anyone should author a book, obviously it should be I.

But oh, how the word "book" seduces, like so much rhino horn. I'm quite sure that in my conversations with the publisher, there were other words besides "book," but all I heard was "book." All I knew about the publisher amounted to a website and his familiarity with my work writing for a cult television show.

But what more did a *writer* need, really? Yes, I would write a book. I would give the world my Average Regional Novelette.

So I took a month or two and wrote. I wrote about some of my experiences living with my parents when I should have long been on my own; I wrote about trying to live in New York City; I wrote about my family, my friends, my life. After a few months of this—and watching Judge Judy whilst fretting about the deadline (just like a *real* writer!)—I submitted the manuscript to the publisher. Soon afterwards, I received my copy in the mail.

It is said that everyone has at least one good book in them. It turns out I had a glorified pamphlet with lots of typos in me. The thing was about the size of a brochure, despite the several thousands of wonderful words I'd scribed. My first mistake: I'd no idea how the word count would translate into actual book pages, and I thought ten thousand would be plenty. I didn't want to overwhelm both possible readers! Even then I thought it'd probably have to come out in volumes, divided up much like Will Durant's *The Story of Civilization*.

Moreover, the cover design simply did not jibe with the contents and the font had been enlarged to 14-point, perhaps to increase the already small page count. I flipped the pages. None of the proofreading corrections had been made. It was full of errors, and one paragraph—if I may be so bold as to refer to the grouping of words as such—was repeated in its entirety. In one iteration, even my name was spelled wrong. Practically in tears, I drew this to the attention of the publisher. "But we fact-checked it!" he insisted.

Aside from that, none of this was the poor fellow's fault. He'd given me an opportunity and after I submitted the flimsy manuscript, I figured everyone else knew what they were doing—at least more than I did. Once again, I'd gone off half-cocked, maybe a little afraid to truly commit to something I really wanted.

I was mortified, crushed. There were maybe a couple hundred copies of this disaster, but I wanted to pretend it never happened. The publisher had other ideas, and he was excited about the promotional opportunities. He called one day and asked out of the blue, "How do you feel about Greyhound buses?"

I'm about as deep as a koi pond and Greyhound buses are but one of the myriad things I'd never considered, either in the abstract or the specific. If pressed, I'd have to say that I feel rather neutral about bus transportation. He went on: "Greyhound has a deal where you can travel across country—unlimited—for $99!! This would be a perfect way to promote the book!"

My friend Lorna has had much success as a novelist, and she tells of being flown in for readings at bookstores or to lead book-club discussions, ferried about in town cars and wrangled by assistants to make sure her every need is accommodated. I envisioned myself making my way from small town to small town on a bus with boxes of my booklet in tow. You know, small towns where buses stop but bookstores no longer exist. Would I go door to door? Would I have a tent show, perhaps? Would I set up a table outside the local 7-Eleven? Would I give home book parties in every county?

It became my secret shame.

Except it wasn't entirely a secret. The *thing* still exists. People have actually purchased the little booklet. Although it is no longer available, thankfully, people write me every now and then with a variety of comments—and not all of them bad. Sometimes I'll meet people who want it signed, which means I have to look them—and the damn thing—in the eye. I have to face it in all its ragged, clumsy existence. And in owning up to failure, I wonder if maybe everything is trial and error. Sure, I'm a gifted speller and sometimes I can distinguish a noun from a verb. Beyond that, it always feels like jumping in fresh, doing my best and hoping for the best. Isn't it the same for all of us, no matter what the endeavor, no matter how many times we've tried?

Sometime later, a dear friend sent me this from novelist Robert Cormier: "The beautiful part of writing is that you don't have to get it right the first time, unlike, say, a brain surgeon."

So here I go again. Some new stories, some old stories. My do-over. A mulligan. A slim volume still, but there are fewer typos and my name is spelled right. I think.

And all for you, my little taco chip you. ❧

The Crush

When I was but a slip of a girl (okay, I've never been a 'slip of a girl' but I've always wanted to be referred to in that manner, so I've gone ahead and done so)… Anyway, when I was but in my teens, I saved all my earnings from babysitting and took my first airplane ride to St. Louis, Missouri, to visit my oldest sister Julie and her brand new husband Rick for the Thanksgiving holiday.

I had a bit of a crush on my brother-in-law. He and Julie had gotten married the previous summer, and he was the first in-law in our family, an older man at 22, and he was really cute and funny and smart. I was a shy, quiet teenager, and when I was around Rick the awkwardness went full tilt: I somehow managed to be both tongue-tied *and* overly talkative. I laughed too quickly and too loudly at any joke he made, my amusement manifesting itself as a harsh, loud, chopping, *Hahaahahahahaa!*

My siblings mocked me, making me cry and journal endlessly—which made for more teasing from my hardscrabble siblings about how annoyingly "sensitive" I was. So what if I swooned over the beauty of Cat Stevens lyrics, so what if I cried when horses got injured in Westerns (the cowboys, on the other hand, had brought it on themselves), and so what if I rescued ants from certain death in the driveway and moved them to the lawn where they could lead happier lives in a more bucolic setting? I *still* managed to find time to write poetry about the evils of mankind.

I thought myself quite the world traveler and managed to "name drop" my trip at every possible turn, thinking my classmates would find me oh-so-continental, jetting off to St. Louis. I sewed myself a stylish pair of plaid polyester pants—not just bell bottoms, *elephant* bells—for my very first airplane ride. It was important that Rick realize I was not the same clumsy, bashful girl who'd been a bridesmaid at his wedding three months earlier. I also decided that I needed to assure Rick that he had married well, and to that end, I planned to impress him with my vast knowledge of all things Crosby, Stills & Nash. I was a huge fan of the musical trio, and quite familiar with them, if I do say so myself. I wanted Rick to know that he could count on at least one member of this family having all the Crosby, Stills & Nash-based information he might ever need.

On the other hand, I had less expertise in the *and Young* oeuvre, and my stomach was in knots as I readied myself for the visit, hoping, praying that Crosby, Stills, Nash *and Young* would never come up. To complicate matters, I had a mad crush on Stephen Stills. What if Rick discovered that I was platonically cheating on him with another unattainable fellow? I hadn't even packed my Samsonite and already the trip was fraught with disaster, like a plum pimple.

I was awestruck by Julie and Rick's efficiency apartment. It was in a raggedy part of town, the three tiny rooms were worn and threadbare, the smell of years of cooking in the old building lingered in the halls, they had a giant wooden cable spool for a coffee table—and it all was the coolest thing I'd ever seen. And—get this—their bed was in the dining room. They were too cool to even have a bedroom.

Julie and Rick squired me all around the city for those three days. There was the Arch, museums, barbecue, the waterfront. Things were going well. I managed to make offhand yet erudite remarks about Crosby, Stills & Nash, no matter how unrelated to the topic at hand. I was enjoying being so urbane, so very sophisticated. One afternoon was spent shopping a row of grungy antique stores and warehouses-*cum* thrift shops, after which we called it a day and piled into the hosts' old station wagon. Rick captained us down the freeway back home, and I was in the back seat, *raconteur*ing and *bon vivant*ing away.

'Twas then I happened to feel something in my pants, a bump at the meeting place of thigh and hip. My hands had been folded in my lap and just happened to brush across this odd bumpy thing. Now, I was a somewhat lumpy teenager but this was a heretofore unknown lump, and I patted it and surreptitiously felt along its contours. I shifted to the right so Rick couldn't see me in the rear-view mirror, and I carefully unzipped my pants a bit. A strange, long, thin, furry, tail-like thing poked out between the zipper. I said, trying to maintain composure, "Um, excuse me, there's something furry in my pants."

Julie glanced over the seat to see me spread-eagled, pressed against the back seat with pants flayed open and whatever it was sticking out of a unzipped zipper. I, on the other hand, was doing my best to appear *nonchalant*.

She screamed. She threw herself against the door as if trying to press her way out, and flailed wildly (this was before the whole seat-belt thing caught on). She was virtually standing as she jiggled the door handle in desperation. She shrieked, "Pull over, ohmygod, pull over!"

Rick skidded into an empty church parking lot, and the car had barely slowed before before Julie flung open the door and staggered across the parking lot, wailing. (She can be high-strung.)

Now Rick looked over the seat. I think we both knew that all the Crosby, Stills & Nash information in the world couldn't get us out of this one. I hoped I was wearing nice underpants—I couldn't bear to look down and check. I watched as Rick wriggled his hand carefully into a leather glove, like a surgeon, and leaned over the seat to grasp the tail-like thing and pluck out a dead mouse.

I shit you not.

We drove home in silence, all three of us duly traumatized. I had been sleeping on the couch but that night, we three of us all got in bed together. I lay in the middle and none of us slept. In retrospect, I realize that Julie and Rick seemed light-years older than I, but they were still pretty much kids themselves, and certainly unprepared to find a dead mouse in someone's pants. (But then, who *is*?) In a long-distance call, my father, a farm kid from way back, said that it was not unusual for mice to run up people's legs—they panic when they're disturbed, and we'd been rummaging around in old buildings. With my bell-bottom pants, well, I was a stylish mousetrap just waiting to happen. More than twenty-five years later, my siblings never fail to point out that the mouse had been alive when it entered my pants, and I unwittingly and accidentally had been its undoing, and they threaten to notify PETA.

I am happy to say that all my Crosby, Stills & Nash information worked, as Julie and Rick are still married. Rick was the first man to see my underpants. I have always loved him, but that—that is a special bond between us, and one that Stephen Stills can never lay claim to. ❧

No Ordinary Girl:
The Mayor's Daughter

Many people do not realize that I come from a political family, nor do many care. But it is true: I am no ordinary citizen of these States United.

You see, in the early 1960s my father was the mayor of Circle Pines, Minnesota, a small town north of the Twin Cities of Minneapolis and St. Paul. At that time, the small cooperative village was a bustling hub of fur trapping, whaling and Turkish rug making, and for two years Daddy presided over a few thousand or so Circle Pinians (or "Pinites" or "Piners"—the matter has never been settled).

Mother, my four siblings and I had many duties as the First Family of Circle Pines. Our primary civic responsibilities, as with every political dynasty from the Roosevelts to the Kennedys, were to refrain from picking teeth, noses or fights in public. There were the ribbon-cutting ceremonies at the opening of the brand new Dairy Queen, and the presenting of the ceremonial key to the city to visiting dignitaries, like the mayor of nearby Blaine. One might think that this jet-setting life was a whirlwind of glamour—but one might not be aware of the disaster that befell the First Family one ordinary summer.

It was customary for the Mayor and his family to ride in the city's Fourth of July parade each year, and tradition dictated that we all ride in a convertible. There were seven of us, as well as the First Dog, the First Hamster and the First Guinea Pig, so that was rather difficult unless we stacked ourselves. In the past this had proven injurious to those on the bottom of the stack, as we were all rather large of build. (My sister still suffers from the aftereffects of a devastating lap injury.) Parade organizers arrived at an ingenious solution: that year, the entire family rode in the back of the utility van our neighbor Roy Rasmussen used for his carpet installation business.

July 4 dawned bright and clear, and we were awfully excited to share in the celebration of our nation's birthday as we crowded into the cargo hold of the van. Roy secured the door behind us, and we arranged ourselves around rolls of then-trendy beige carpeting. Roy began driving and we could hear the muffled sounds of the marching band and the Shriners revving their tiny motorcycles as we motor-paraded down Main Street. The truck seemed barely able to make its way through the throng of several half dozens of Daddy's loyal populace as they waved and cheered their beloved First Family, although I take this on faith, as there were no windows in the back of the truck.

Amidst what we assumed to be a jubilant celebration, my seven-year-old brother was overcome by all the excitement and vigorously threw a handful of candy to the unwitting crowd. He knew not his own strength and the maelstrom of Jolly Ranchers, Hershey's Kisses, and Bit-O-Honeys ricocheted off the walls of the truck, painfully peppering us like horrible bullets of sugar. Would that it had ended there.

The hail of sweets ceased and in one brief, silent moment we realized: the treats lay at our feet! Ever aware of their duty to the public,

Mayor Daddy and Mrs. Mayor Mother bravely kept waving. But we children, never ones to pass up victuals of any kind, most especially sweets, found ourselves in a donnybrook that European soccer fans could only dream of. Yes, when it came to foodstuffs of any kind, it was every man for himself, and good luck and Godspeed to any delectable that found itself vulnerable. Even now, some forty years later, I cannot forget the poor, wayward Skittle that rolled to a stop in the corner of the van under a bucket of carpet glue.

Eventually the screams subsided and the sobbing waned, and we discovered that one of my brothers had incurred a wound so awful it required one of those tiny Band-Aids that you never use from the assortment box. My sister broke a finger. Thankfully the crowds were quite unaware of the grisly chaos inside the truck—and they never knew that Daddy courageously completed his term with a chocolate gold-foil-wrapped coin inextricably lodged in his nasal passages.

The incident might have passed unnoticed and become a dark secret buried deep in the vaults of our family history but for the outcry among the citizenry when the parade was over and they were left empty-handed, candy-wise. An investigation was launched, and much shame came unto the House of Pehl. Soon after, Daddy was ousted from power in a terrible military coup. (Historians believe that the local National Guard unit was merely on weekend maneuvers and Daddy completely misread the situation.)

Be that as it may. That was a long time ago and the wounds have healed, though I still have the fillings from the cavities that the candy wrought. And in the summer months, I so want to love a parade, but I can never look at those weird taffy things wrapped in wax paper without sadly recalling that day in our nation's history and weeping for what might have been. ❧

The Two Mrs. McDowalls

The first love of my life was Roderick Andrew Anthony Jude McDowall.

Roddy McDowall was a British child actor of the 1940s, featured in films like *My Friend Flicka*, *How Green Was My Valley*, and of course, *Tuna Clipper*. He had big brown eyes, jug ears, a sensitive countenance and a romantic English accent.

My best friend Michelle introduced me to him in the mid-Seventies, when she and I were in junior high. She'd discovered his existence in a late-night television airing of *How Green Was My Valley*, in which he'd starred when he was eleven or so. He'd worked steadily as an actor since his childhood fame, but at that time he was experiencing a renewed fame for the *Planet of the Apes* television series, which was fresh off the *Planet of the Apes* movies, films in which I thought him totally hot, even in complete monkey drag.

Michelle was short, red-haired, and fearless. I was tall, pillowy of form, and wary of everything. We did not have the straight teeth or slim bodies or perfect skin that was the currency in junior high. Our hair could not be styled into the bounteous, fountain-y Farrah Fawcett 'do of the time, we never made the cheerleading squad, and we were aggressively average in our studies. None of this mattered: we had Roddy McDowall.

He was significantly older—and significantly less popular—than the standard heartthrobs of the day, your Scott Baios, Leif Garretts, Mark Hamills. Oh, how much more wordly were we than our peers with their silly, prosaic crushes. It takes a special kind of devotion to be in love with a rather obscure, nondescript middle-aged movie actor of indeterminate talent and sexuality. It's a lot harder to keep up that sort of relationship when the object of your affections doesn't appear in a large color poster to be affixed to the ceiling over your bed.

Every week with all our babysitting money, Michelle and I would go to the drugstore in our small town to get *TV Guide* and *People* on the day they hit the stands, even waiting for the boxes to be unpacked. *People* had recently debuted, and I secretly believed that it had been launched for the sole purpose of distributing Roddy McDowall information to the hungry masses: i.e., Michelle and me.

Nearly every afternoon after an interminable daily bout of junior high, we'd trudge to Michelle's house, where we'd sit on the floor of the tiny bedroom she shared with her sisters. We were squeezed between the beds, and magazines swirled around us like a fancy skirt as we pored over them for anything remotely related to Roddy McDowall.

I'd scour the *TV Guide*. There was *Planet of the Apes* on Friday night and there was always the possibility he might be a guest star on *Night Gallery* or *The Carol Burnett Show*. It got so I'd have memorized each week's *Guide* and I could tell my family what was on the tube at any given time on any given day, off the top of my head.

We examined the tabloids for anything about his love life. We knew he was friends with Elizabeth Taylor—but *just* friends. We hoped. She would be a lot of woman to compete with when we moved to Hollywood after completing 9th grade to live with him. The plan was we'd be adopted by him. We never hammered out the details about the adoption—like what to do with the parents we already had. Our paths would miraculously cross some way, somehow, and once he met us, he would realize we were the missing pieces of his life. Michelle and I could stay together as best friends: in fact, we would be sisters.

These ideas snowballed into an obsession about all the potential awkwardness as Roddy McDowall's daughters. For instance, what if we couldn't drop the habit of calling him *Mr. McDowall*? We practiced possible scenarios with all earnestness. I would be Roddy McDowall and Michelle would be Michelle. She would "accidentally" call me Roddy. I would touch her shoulder gently, look into her eyes with as much avuncularity as a 14-year-old girl could muster, and say, "Hey, honey—it's 'Dad.'" Michelle would grin a grateful grin and say, "Okay —*Dad*." I'd reply gently, like a good TV dad, "I like the way that sounds." Michelle would nod and say, "Me too"—and with a knowing, grateful look, add, "*Dad*."

When it was her turn to be Roddy McDowall and I the daughter, I would begin to say, "Hey, Mr. McDow—" and she'd give me a playfully remonstrative look, wherein I'd realized what I'd almost said. Sheepish yet beaming, I'd correct myself. "I mean *Dad*." Michelle-Roddy would reply, "Yes, *daughter*?"—and smile lovingly at me.

Over the two years or so of our crush, we matured a little bit. We began to discuss the possibility of marriage. Since no wife or girlfriend was ever mentioned in any reports of him, we felt we had as good a chance as anyone. I was nervous about the possibility of sex with him (after our wedding, of course), mostly because I was unclear about what it entailed. My mother had nervously read to me a Catholic pamphlet about a man loving a woman very much and in whom he planted a seed when they were married. I, a simpleton and literalist, thought she had sat me down to talk about sex.

Michelle and I decided that once we moved to Hollywood, we would let Roddy choose between us for his bride. No hard feelings, in fact, we wished each other the best. Then, after one of us married him, we'd adopt the other—who would be there to coach the chosen one through the wedding night. Trust me, it all worked out seamlessly in our dreams.

Some twenty-five years later I was writing for *Mystery Science Theater 3000* and one of the episodes we aired was the 1978 film *Laserblast*, in which Roddy McDowall played an evil corporate executive. As we watched the movie and wrote the jokes, I stared at his face on the screen. I wondered if he'd gotten the fan letter Michelle and I labored over; I wondered if he ever knew that I'd written a letter of outrage to the daily paper when it had misspelled his name; I wondered if he was a good actor or not—it was so hard for me to tell through my rose-colored glasses.

Michelle and I had fallen out of touch, our lives having diverged after high school. Roddy died in October of 1998, and his obituary read that "the actor, who never married" had succumbed to cancer. There was no girlfriend nor "long-time companion" mentioned, now that I realized that there was such a thing as "long-time companions." Still, I couldn't help but wonder if Michelle and I might have changed the course of his life. One can dream, can't one? ✣

Postcards from China

More than halfway into a
16-hour flight to China I
remembered: I don't like
Chinese food.

I am between jobs. Again. Friend
Peter and I discovered a really
cheap, last-minute package tour
to Beijing. Why not? I shall tend
to any filing and/or alphabetizing
emergencies upon my return.
A few days later, we're off
on our grand adventure. But I
think about what I'll eat. Trying
not to worry: every culture has
some version of candy.

A tour of the Old City with an ad hoc group, Americans all. Guide shows us huge iconographic picture of Mao in Tiananmen Square, guy from Wisconsin points to it and asks the tour guide, "So, is that guy your king or something?" Hoorah! I won't be the biggest idiot in the group!

Very, very strange. Everywhere we go, I am by approached by denizens wanting to take my photograph. At the Great Wall, a young woman who wants a picture of me with her friend is laughing so hard can barely hold the camera steady. It's really humiliating to not be in on the joke. I'm not the only caucasian here, not by a long shot. Peter points out matter-of-factly I'm possibly the whitest person on the planet. I imagine families throughout China pulling out their photo albums on a Sunday afternoon, poring over the pictures and reminiscing fondly, and then trying to explain the big white girl standing there with them like Zelig.

My Friend Sandy Once Told Me,
Wrestling Touches Us All

*An Aphorism To Be Needlepointed On A Decorative
Pillow If There Ever Was One*

M y father supported our family as a public accountant, and he had
his own income tax business. In my growing-up years, I rarely saw
him from January til April, for this was "tax season." He left for work in
the early morning dark, and returned late at night in the same darkness.

To walk into his place of business was to smell the perfume of the office assistants, perhaps the daring Tabu or something by Prince Match-
abelli, entwined with the burnt, inky scent of the copy machine. Desks
and work spaces were sprinkled with the tiny, rubbery corkscrew rubble
of erasers rubbed vigorously in a time when everything was done by
hand in pencil. There was the persistent rhythm of various adding ma-
chines and typewriters, underscored by the easy-listening station playing
on the boxy clock radio above the receptionist's desk. And paper. So

much paper. Paper and files and paper and notes everywhere.

Behind his large, steel desk, my father would have a mechanical pencil in one hand while the fingers of the other hand danced on the keys of the adding machine, which churned out a white curling roll of paper that covered the floor as if a bookkeeping parade had passed through. He could simultaneously carry on conversations with his clients, many of whom were neighbors in our small town, not even having to look at the keyboard.

For my father, numbers added up sideways and up and down their rows and columns. For me, there was a mystique to all this—I, whom fate had deigned to cruelly smite with dyscalculia (a condition I share with Mary Tyler Moore). It all was especially thrilling because of one thing in particular: a certain Bert Smith.

You may know him as Stan Kowalski, or perhaps Krusher Kowalski, aka Killer Kowalski. Yes, he of the World Wide Wrestling Federation— The Big K, the self-same Krippler Karl Kovacs. Favorite moves: eye gouge. Notable feuds: Dick the Bruiser and Crusher Lisowski. Accountant: Jerry Pehl. Even professional wrestlers had to get their taxes done.

Krusher Kowalski was famous in our household. On most Saturday mornings in the "off" season, my dad would watch wrestling on the local television channel. He'd sit with a Hamms beer, feet up on the ottoman, peering through black-framed glasses, all a brief respite from two jobs and five kids. Krusher was just one of the wrestlers declaring blood feuds with the other wrestlers, and intimidating the announcer with threats. It always made me uneasy even though my dad assured me it was all just a put-on.

Sometimes I'd get to go with my dad to the office on Saturday mornings to "help" (read: daydream and make art projects on the copy machine. Besides, if my dyscalculia had flared up, I really was unable to attend to anything). Every year during tax season, Krusher would come to Pop's small office in a small, nondescript strip mall which also housed the local insurance agency, the little library and the weekly paper, *The Circulating Pines*. I always hoped that *that* Saturday, *my* Saturday, would be the day Killer was to come in for his tax appointment. My dad rubbed elbows with wrestlers, for cryin' out loud, and I wanted a piece of the action.

I imagined that, what with being pressed for time, Krusher would wear his wrestling singlet, under his parka or heavy coat for Minnesota winters, his legs be-tighted and feet in wrestling booties. I so wanted Killer Kowalski to be sitting in my father's little office, discussing amortizations and deductions and saved receipts, so I could casually name-drop him at school on Monday.

I wanted to know: Did my father call him Bert? Or perhaps Mr. Killer? I had a precocious grasp of the argot and an obsession with logistics. I wondered, did the wrestling federation issue W-2s? Or are wrasslin' earnings considered 1099 income? Was the vicious heel tag team he formed with Tiny Mills, known as "Murder Incorporated," *officially* incorporated in the eyes of the IRS?

None of this was my business, my father told me, but still I hoped, still I imagined some drama unfolding one day in the persistently beige office. What if my father recommended to The Krusher that he keep better track of his receipts next year? Would this set off the hair-trigger temper that I imagined? Perhaps The Krusher would lunge over the desk, his nut-cup clanking against the metal desk top and skewing paperwork to and fro in the air; wherein Krippler Karl would issue a piledriver and a choke-slam on my pop. My father would clutch his glasses to keep them from being broken in the midst of a front facelock, because, good god, we could not afford to replace spectacles and he'd worn the same pair for at least a decade. Maybe, as I sat at the reception desk doodling *Mrs. Roddy McDowall* on the appointment pad, I'd hear my dad cry out from behind the office door, "Krippler, Krippler! It's the IRS's rules, not mine!"

I wonder if I wanted this brush with celebrity as much for my father as myself. He worked long hours in an office, and maybe I hoped for some break in the routine, a pop of excitement in his life. To ask him about it now, Mr. Smith was just a regular guy, who, after retiring from wrestling, ran for a spot on the local school board. He was just the sum of his adjusted gross income and deductions, all columns and rows, calculations that balanced tidily up and down and left to right. And for my dad, that was always pretty good. ✎

To All The Companies With
Whom I Was Never Employed:
You're Welcome

Very few people know that every single day of my life, I wage a courageous battle with a chronic, debilitating condition. The time has come to be honest: for years, I have struggled with early on-set ergasiophobia. I know you must be in shock as you read this, as I have always appeared so hale and hearty.

Yes, I suffer from a crippling fear of work. I have decided to be honest about the matter in hopes that somehow I can help others. Why, I hardly have time to write this, as I am organizing a walk to raise awareness of ergasiophobia. I mean, I *would* organize a walk or design a different color lapel ribbon—but for the ergasiophobia.

Oh, I've tried having jobs. And tried. And tried and tried and tried some more. My first job out of college was with K-Tel International.

K-Tel is famous for making compilation albums, and I worked in the media department, sending out slides and ads to TV stations in Ye Olden Dayes before everything was digitized. I thought I was in the music industry. My boss smoked Tiparillos and had really long toenails, and she wore sandals even in winter to show off those long, pedicured toenails. I was laid off when K-Tel went bankrupt.

My problem wasn't so much *getting* hired. It was the *staying* hired that proved nigh impossible. There were jobs with advertising agencies, an orchestra, a non-profit arts organization, and almost every company in the Tri-State region. I just kept getting fired or laid off, or both if the company was particularly vindictive. Several companies went bankrupt or went out of business. I tried not to see myself as the only common denominator.

To be frank, I also got fired from several jobs. I was a perfect storm of idiocy, immaturity and daydreamcy. There was also my "attitude," as my superiors referred to it. To wit: I got fired from a secretarial job that I hated because everybody acted like I was their secretary or something.

In one particular secretarial position for a non-profit, I typed lots of letters and memos to staff and the Board of Directors. Always trying to take a creative approach to my work, I'd change the names of the addressees into expletives to amuse myself. I always changed the names back before my boss proofread them. *Usually* always. Until that fateful memo that was overlooked, and the "noms des expletives" went out to everyone. I was fired, and rightfully so, but unfortunately before I had an opportunity to apologize to Bill Fuckson. If there's any takeaway to be had from this modest little volume, please learn from my mistake.

It happened that a like-minded colleague at K-Tel dragged me to an open mic one night. It was at a pub in Uptown Minneapolis, the kind with peanut shells covering the floor which was oh-so-*au courant* those days, and that night there were more comedians than audience members. I remembered about one minute of the three I'd tried to memorize. Whatever it was, it worked. I did a couple of more open stages and started getting booked right away. This was during the comedy boom of the mid-to-late '80s, and every bar, every nightclub, every church basement, was putting a microphone in the corner of the establishment and calling it a comedy club as a means to sell more beer.

I'd become rather well-known in the Twin Cities for my postmodern, deconstructionist interpretation of employment, and I started temping to supplement the sparse income. Temping was a godsend: there were no office politics to navigate, and the getting fired was already built in! It was so *liberating*!

But I was shocked to discover that the temp agency loved me. I was quiet, which was mistaken for efficiency, and I showed up for work, which was mistaken for aptitude. I worked at companies where you were considered a libertine if you wore separates, and people were astonished if you showed the slightest glimmer of intelligence at all. For one mundane clerical assignment, a woman trained me by pointing to office equipment.

"So, um, that is, the um...ya know..." she'd stammer.

I jumped in. "Copier?"

She was so pleased. She said, "You're catching on real quick!"

At another assignment, a harried, impatient fellow showed me a stack of filing that needed to be done, and asked me if I was "familiar with the alphabet."

I often wondered how my temporary colleagues got *their* jobs. Once I worked with a woman who was having sinus problems, and one morning she informed me she was leaving early to see the doctor about her "nosal passages."

I wasn't sure I'd heard right.

"Nosal passages?" I asked.

She blinked impatiently and tapped the side of her nose with irritation. "Yes," she said sternly. "*Nosal* passages!"

I rose through the ranks of temping, or at least I think I must have, for I was named Employee of the Month in March 1990. I'll never forget that day. I was awarded a plaque which showed, embossed in metal, a slim, long-legged career woman striding purposefully into her destiny. I wept with sorrow. I had excelled at something I did not wish to, and the lady on the plaque clearly didn't know I was merely stumbling forward, and flailing onward. ❧

I Lived With My Parents

I lay in a child's trundle bed and stared up at the ceiling in the small room that also served as my father's home office. Above me I heard the *vrrrm-vrrrrrrrm* of my parents' massive adjustable beds as they tried to find a good angle by which to watch television. They were watching *Survivor*. This I knew because the volume was cranked as loud as it could go. Someone was being voted off the island. Me, I was forty years old, broke, without a job or car, and living in my parents' basement in the suburbs.

After a certain age, you're just not supposed to live with your parents. I'd be hard pressed to articulate why exactly—I'm guessing it might have something to do with homicide laws.

My friends, cousins, the clerk at the grocery store, would casually say, "Hi, how are you?"

I wanted to shriek: "*How the hell do you think I am?!*"

The *plan* was that after *Mystery Science Theater 3000* was canceled and I'd be out of a job, I would sell all my worldly possessions and travel the world with nothing but a backpack and pluck—and hopefully some decent hand lotion. When I returned I would move in with my parents in their basement for a few months while I figured out the next phase of my life.

It's very unnerving when plans go the way you planned.

My mother soothed me, "You're not *living* here—you're just *staying* here until you move to New York!"

"Besides, we *like* having you here!"

After a pause, she'd add, "And it's not a basement—it's a 'lower level.'" She was proud of the fact that the basement had been finished off to look somewhat less basement-like.

You know how if you have a decent, loving, normal-ish relationship with your Mom and Dad, you think you know them? Listen, mister, you *don't*. It'd been more than twenty years since I'd lived with them, and I was a grownup now, a grownup in a parent/child position. So they weren't just parents anymore—they were fellow adults. With personalities that they'd they'd probably always had, but I was too self-absorbed to notice. I was a Dian Fossey observing these familiar yet new creatures.

My father Jerry is tall, and every morning he gets up in a good mood. He has crackling blue eyes and big pink cheeks that suggest a retired cherub. He sneezes in enormous roars that you can feel through the house, cataclysmic and undulating, a booming "*Rrrrwhaahahaaa!*" My father thinks Benny Hill is one of the brilliant comic minds of this or any generation, and will often describe particular episodes of the program to me in excruciating detail.

My mother Dorothy is short, and gets quite annoyed by my father's unfailing good mood. She gets cold easily and when she bundles up against the Minnesota weather; there are so many shirts, sets of long underwear, pants, sweaters, coats, mittens, and scarves on her that she looks like a diabolical experiment, a human head transplanted on top of a pile of laundry.

Dorothy makes weekly trips to the Wonder Bread Outlet bakery—yes, there is such a place—and she buys lots of day-old, marked-down bread to be put in the extra freezer in the garage. The bread might be eaten in a couple of weeks or a couple of years. *It doesn't matter once it's frozen*, she insisted, *it's just as good as fresh*. My mother, ever the bargain shopper, would die happy if she could find a deal on used bread.

Every week she invited me upstairs for Sunday dinner. The recipes invariably involved some permutation of frozen hash browns and cream of mushroom soup. In my parents' house, sour cream is considered a side dish and butter is a spice to be used liberally. They salt everything: sausage, salad, fruit. Before they've tasted it. And they'll keep salting the same food, until there's one bite of food left on the plate, which upon closer examination is a just a mound of salted salt.

One of my mother's culinary experimentations was a fudge recipe which called for Velveeta cheese. I was curious how one came out ahead using a processed cheese product in a fudge recipe—was it supposed to be a fudge *con queso* perhaps? Dorothy explained that it was supposed to make the fudge creamier. In fact, it tasted like viscous old carpet.

Sometimes I'd happen across my parents standing at the kitchen window, side by side, gazing out onto the busy residential street. They'd lock in on the neighbors or passers-by, and comment to each other in terse, conspiratorial voices.

"Hey, Dot!" my father would hiss at my mother. "Look at that guy!"

After a few seconds of looking at that guy, she'd concur, marveling: "Oh, would you *look* at that guy?!"

They'd look at that guy for some time, heads moving in unison. Heaven knows what it was about *that guy*. With a *pffff*, Mom would shake her head. "Check out Mr. Cool."

Jerry would concur. "Yep. There goes Mr. Cool."

To them, "Mr. Cool" was usually some fellow who might be parading around in a t-shirt with a rock band logo, or perhaps driving a late model car in a color other than blue or black.

This was their American dream, I suppose—all Velveeta and bread and television and Mr. Cools of it. My father had often worked two jobs over the course of my childhood, and owned several businesses. My mother hadn't gotten her driver's license until she was in her mid-twenties, already raising five young children, and herself had taken part-time jobs and owned her own businesses. Who was I to begrudge them?

Even if they had eight recliners. Eight recliners throughout their modest two-story. Dorothy and Jerry Pehl had earned the right to recline whenever and wherever they wanted. The months I lived with them, I grew used to talking to them at a 45-degree angle, the incline at which they'd conduct their lives, read, watch TV, talk on the phone, eat dinner. Once I was startled to see my mom upright. I'd forgotten she could be so vertical.

Still I worried when I found almost fifty plastic drinking cups from Days Inn, accumulated from their road trips and still wrapped in their hygienic cellophane. I knew my parents weren't necessarily rich but I assumed they were doing all right. Did they desperately want for containers from which to consume beverages? Or did they know something I didn't? They'd lived through the Depression and the Cold War. Who knows, maybe they were preparing for some apocalyptic shortage of cups, or bread, or recliners.

And no one was more supportive as I waited out those days in their lower level, dejected and aimless. One, two, three months passed as I tried to find a job in New York and plan the move. They brainstormed. One day my mother, horizontal in a recliner, with tweezers in one hand and a small magnifying mirror as she fought her Waterloo with the goat-hairs on her chin, said out of nowhere, "Have you ever thought of being a news anchor on CNN?"

"No." I said. "Why?"

"Well, all those anchors have such nice skin—and you have a beautiful complexion!"

My father had a eureka moment. "Why don't you go to Las Vegas and be in a show? You'd be so good!" I didn't know if he thought I should be a magician's assistant or a middle-age topless showgirl or star in some extravaganza with tigers but it was indeed an idea.

I guess.

I tried to be as optimistic as they were, and I hoped and prayed that my mother was right, that I wasn't really *living* there, that this was just a transition, but how would you ever know for sure? As month number three unfolded in my parents' lower level, me still staring up at their bedroom ceiling, I began to wonder: what if I woke up in three or seven or twenty years and it dawned on me that my plans to move just sort of got away from me? There I'd be: I'd have collected thousands of mini-bars of soap and plastic cups from motels and I'd be wearing two or three housedresses at once and nobody would know if my parents had actually died or not, they were just never seen again and I'd be salting my food, ice cream and canned pears and hoarding mugs and tumblers just in case, and I'd declare to the stranger sitting next to me on the bus, "there goes Mr. Cool."

These kinds of things just sneak up on ya. ❧

Big Baby

There have been times when I have been, well, um, kind of righteous. I have, on occasion, confronted smokers who flick their cigarettes to the ground by picking up the butt and haughtily returning it to them, declaring, "I think you dropped something." I have raised a modest ruckus or two when someone cuts in front of another in a checkout line. I will return junk mail with a "Refused—return to sender" scribbled on it, and though I know it does little good, I just don't want to be the one to throw it in a landfill. If *I* don't straighten out the world, *who* will?

In the few months that I lived with my parents, my mother was having arthritis in her knees and replacement surgery was imminent. With that, her heart surgery and all manner of additional structural renovations, she'd pretty much become the Six Million Dollar Grandma. (We can make you stronger, faster, get you to the senior citizen buffet earlier!) For years I'd watched as the pain in her legs grew worse and downright debilitating. It got to the point that even the most minor outing turned into an expedition that required judicious planning.

She finally broke down and got a handicapped parking card. Even a few yards made a lot of difference when she was trying to get somewhere, and being able to rely on convenient parking gave her a greater sense of independence and control of her life. And when the little blue placard arrived in the mail…

I immediately deputized myself in the name of truth and justice where parking was concerned. I was constantly on the lookout for ne'er-do-wells using the specially designated spots when they oughtn't. If a permit wasn't visible, I'd ask to see it. (I even went so far as to shoot people nasty looks.) Once I alerted a mall security guard when I spotted a scofflaw. Yes, wherever honest parking was in peril, Mary Jo Pehl was there.

And then…

I began hanging out with my mother. A lot. I would go with her just to be able to park close to whatever establishment we deigned to visit. During those few months I spent more time with her than I had my whole life. I didn't *want* to go to Costco, I didn't *want* to go to Over 55 Water Aerobics, I didn't *want* to go to Old County Buffet, but a secret thrill coursed through me when we'd pull up just a few feet from the door. I became sort of heady with power. (I guess I was just lucky there was no small nearby country begging to be annexed. Who knows how I may have wielded my perceived might.) Yes, I was riding my mother's incapacitated coattails.

One day she asked me to run to the drugstore to pick up some medications. I played it cool, but I couldn't wait to park. Hopping in her car, I drove up to the strip mall and breezily pulled into the sole handicapped-parking space, whereupon I hooked the placard on the rearview mirror and opened the door. At that moment, a car with a handicapped parking card pulled next to me.

I froze. Humiliation rigor-mortification set in. I, entirely able-bodied, was doing a bad, wrong thing and I'm Midwestern and Catholic, and I always feel like I'm doing something bad and wrong, even when it's something routine and legal, like folding laundry.

I tried to sneak out of the car. By this time the driver had come around to my side where I was overly casually trying to lock the door. One of his pant legs was loose from the knee down.

"Hi," he said. "So, what happened to you?" His tone was merely curious.

I've never been quick on my feet, and I said the only thing that came to mind.

"Had a baby."

But it came out in a weird, tough-guy voice that startled me when I heard myself utter it. You might have thought there was a Marlboro dangling from my lips or that I had "love" and "hate" tattooed on my knuckles or that I'd tell you I'd shot a man in Circle Pines just to watch him die. The closest I've ever come to having a baby was being an aunt. I can barely tell a newborn from a freshly packaged chicken at the grocery store.

He looked at me quizzically.

"Big one," I added gruffly.

I was digging myself in deeper with a backhoe, and I was thoroughly disgusted with myself. Another unnatural voice came out of me, one gratingly and unnaturally perky.

"And you?" Like I was running for homecoming queen.

He'd been in a terrible car accident.

"I was lucky," he said. "I only lost part of this leg."

Again my voice took over. With a huge smile, I declared loudly "Oh, wow!" As if that were the most exciting news I'd had that day, as if congratulations were in order.

We stood there, maybe hours, maybe seconds, looking at each other. I couldn't walk into the store because I didn't know how a new mother of a large baby should walk so as to warrant a handicapped parking spot.

At long last he shook my hand. "Nice talking to you—you take care of yourself," he said and went on his way. I pretend-hobbled back into my mother's car and sat and cried. I cried because of a stranger's gentleness, I cried for his struggle, and I cried because I discovered I was just as rotten as everyone else.

And because I am Midwestern and Catholic, heretofore I will wear a hair shirt and sleep on a wooden pillow and I will park as far away from every entrance as is possible. And I shall leave everyone in peace. ✎

Postcards from China

We hire a private guide to take us around the city. We visit a large, beautiful park and have cheesy tourist photographs taken of ourselves in traditional Chinese wedding garb. Nearby are four men carrying tourists around in a sedan on poles, carried like a litter. Guide explains Chinese wedding tradition is for bride to be carried in bridal sedan to wedding while others follow singing and playing musical instruments. This replica is for the amusement of the visitors to the park.

The men urge us into the sedan. No way. Pete's always game for anything, and already in the box. I'm shoved in by the fellows. I'm big, it's tiny. I'm half propped against/on Peter's lap, my head at a right angle against the ceiling.

Celebratory fanfare begins. Sedan is raised. Slowly. Very slowly. Looking out the tiny window, we see poles bending. Becomes apparent that there will be no exuberant jostling of us. Fellows try to sing but it's too strenuous—amounts to sort of melodious groans. Through tiny window, we see the men hunched over and straining. A few long minutes later, poor fellows can't even complete circle. We are set down with a thud and a grunt. We pay, thanking them profusely and are on our way.

One of the men calls out to our guide. He sounds proud, triumphant – maybe even boastful? Guide translates for us: Pete and I were the heaviest they'd ever carried. A proud day for everyone.

Matryoshka Dolls

My niece was playing in the bathtub, having the time of her three-year-old life. Her parents had their hands full getting the other kids ready for bed, and I hollered that I'd get Marie out of the tub. She looked up at me from the tepid water.

"But only my mom knows how to wrap me in the towel right," she coolly informed me.

Lately my family has become become overrun by these creatures, these offspring of my brothers and sisters. Each child seems to be fully mammalian, yet an alien of sorts who were wanted but we didn't realize we'd get *them* exactly. Like ordering mystery gifts from a Harriet Carter catalog: the ad declares "For $5.95, we'll pick a special surprise gift for you!" and you get a package filled with stuff but you have no idea what it will be.

The little girl was right, I don't have children of my own, so what do I know from wrapping a towel around a freshly bathed child? I am not part of the infinite matryoshka doll succession of humanity—someone's daughter giving way to another daughter giving way to another daughter, like Russian nesting dolls. I promised to do my best and bring her immediately to her mother so any mistakes could be corrected.

My family loves its babies and is able to maintain a steady inventory. Me, I have known for some time that I cannot have children—if I want to sleep late. Of course, adoption is always a possibility, but I could only seriously consider someone in their 20s or 30s. (Those kids are very hard to place, by the by.) And if they could live elsewhere and support themselves, why, I think that would work out best for everyone involved.

So somehow I have become the overbearing aunt in the family. I don't know how it happened. Suddenly I was forcing kisses on them, getting lipstick on their cheeks and wiping it off with my fingers, and giving them pennies out of my purse, even the 21-year-old. Maybe it's in the aunt DNA. And I was surprised at my proprietary claims which arrived in sudden and unwieldy ways. I made up arbitrary and stringent rules, as if it was any of my business, like busybodily noting that my teen nieces should wear turtlenecks under their strapless prom dresses, or getting pangs of sadness when my nephews became too cool to hug me.

Pregnancy and childbirth are both spellbinding and a little, well, dreadful. It is fascinating that women even *walk* after giving birth. I'd insist on a wheelchair for at least ten years; in fact, I'd probably have to move into assisted living. Come to think of it, I'd probably need a service animal of some sort.

My mother and I have had the same conversation many times over the years. I tell her that what I think I'm really afraid of is the pain. She can remember each of her five pregnancies and labors in great and vivid detail, and she always says, "Oh, but you forget about it right away."

Then she always says, with some exasperation, "And besides, millions of women have done it for millions of years."

To which I always respond, "That doesn't make it right."

My mother had a heart attack a few years ago. A minor one as they go; in fact, when she was being transferred by ambulance from one hospital to another, she had the wherewithal to implore the EMTs to stop at a local Sam's Club for its grand opening, as it was the only day you could get a free membership. I lie not.

Since then, she'd followed doctor's orders to the letter and was doing quite well. Then after one check-up, a nurse from the doctor's office called and left a message on her answering machine. It was the night before Thanksgiving and in a chipper tone, the nurse informed her that the recent tests didn't look so good, but that she could discuss it with the doctor the following week. In that pointy Minnesota accent that seems to be amplified in female health care professionals, the nurse signed off with a breezy, "Now don't let this information ruin your holiday weekend. Bye now!"

It ruined our holiday weekend. No one could think of anything else. My brother, also a nurse, tried to spin the message to sound less ominous. A family friend, an M.D., tried to allay my mother's fears. And despite my advanced medical training as a committed viewer of *Medical Center* and *St. Elsewhere*, I too was at a loss to ease her worries.

She couldn't *not* think of it, and the weekend went on forever. One night as she sat in her recliner, she put her book down and tried fiercely not to cry.

"I'm just not ready to say good-bye to the grandchildren," she said.

And for the first time in my dimly lit life I saw my mother as a woman. I mean, I've always *suspected*, I know I came from somewhere, but in that moment it hit me. She was human. Because you don't always get that about your mother. I realized I was once a baby in her arms. She'd labored alone in a hospital room, as with all my siblings, in the days before fathers were allowed in the delivery room. Did she wonder what creature I was going to be for her? Did she have any idea what she was going to get? Was it then, having had the third child with two more to follow, that she realized she might never be a professional figure skater, weight and talent notwithstanding, now that she and my father were supporting kids and struggling each month to make the $94 mortgage?

The nurse's call was a false alarm that only required a minor change in medications. Months later, I watched my mother with the latest baby. She has always been expert in the way she holds newborns, one hand cradling the head and the other hand under the body so the baby faces her, almost nose-to-nose. She has a way of talking to infants, in a low and caramelly voice. The tiny girl fixed on my mother, riveted, and flailed her scrawny limbs, never taking her eyes away from my mother's lovely face. There was some sort of lock between them with my mother's gentle voodoo. Then and there, they were the only two people in the world.

It's been decades, but I guess only my mother knew how to wrap me in a towel right. After each bath, she'd comb out my hair, turning me around as I stood at her knees dutifully and fluffing up my white blond hair with her elegant fingers. Every time she'd say, "It dries nicer this way." My niece knows her towel-wrapping mother for the artisan she is. ❧

A Bridge Too Far—
Way Too Far

O ne bright April morning I landed at JFK International Airport with everything I owned in three suitcases and I hailed
a shining yellow taxi. My life as a New Yorker had officially begun.

Neither I nor the driver said anything as he loaded my suitcases
into the trunk of the cab. I thought, *Wait! Just because I'm a New
Yorker now doesn't mean I'm going to be impersonal and brusque and
not even greet my fellow human being just because he's in the service
industry!*

I said hello and gave him the address. He asked what brought
me to New York, and I said that I was going to live here. He told
me that he had come from Haiti twenty years ago because he had
always wanted to live in America.

Our lives were so very parallel! Both of us, strangers in a strange land, pursuing our dreams! We chatted. He had an intriguing accent and cute little speech impediment. He introduced himself: Wodney. Such an exotic Haitian name: *Wodney!* I introduced myself, and he said, "Welcome to New York, Mary!" but it came out *Maywee.*

Wodney told me about the big, dangerous city of New York, and he warned that a lot of bad things could happen to me if I wasn't very very careful. He said that I had better be extra careful because a lot of men would want to be my boyfriend. Now, I'd always been a late bloomer and had had very few relationships to that point. Upon hearing this, I settled back in the seat and turned my face to try to hide my excitement at this prospect. I thought, *I'm going to like it here just fine.*

Wodney continued to drive, taking his clipboard and anchoring it on the steering wheel with his left hand. He took a pen in his right hand and began to sketch on the paper, all the while maneuvering through midday New York city traffic.

"You see, Maywee, women have a bwidge." He sketched a stick figure, approximately female-like, and some lines to represent a bridge.

"Now—men are like caws." At the other end of the bridge, he drew a crude vehicle, wheels scrawled beneath the boxy shape.

"Now, a lot of caws always want to cwoss a woman's bwidge," he said, shaking the pen in my direction, then tapping it on the picture he'd just drawn.

Positively enthralled, I leaned my chin on the back of the seat, watching Wodney's face in the rearview mirror. Our eyes met and he said gravely, "Don't let just any man cwoss your bwidge, Maywee." He sternly and repeatedly Xed out the car about to cross the bridge.

We talked and laughed and flirted on the drive to the city, and when he dropped me off we exchanged phone numbers. I had lived in New York for less than an hour, and I already had a boyfriend! *And he had a car!*

He called a few days later, and 'twas then I realized his name was actually Rodney. The following evening he picked me up in the cab, whereupon he presented me with a huge bouquet of flowers. I got to sit in the front seat and we drove to Times Square and it sparkled and shone and I couldn't have been any more in New York City than I was at that very moment and oh, how very cosmopolitan was I in my Spalding Grey perfect moment!

Some time later, Wodney drove me home and we parked in front of my apartment building. He took my hand and assumed a rather professorial air, and he began to expound on his bridge theory. He went on to say that many women had guards at their bridge and only let special cars cross. By now, I'd been in New York over two days and I was kind of jaded. Somewhere amidst the noise of New York, subways rumbling beneath us, dogs barking and cars honking, I swear I heard a metaphor being tortured.

"Take you and me fow instance, Maywee," he said somberly. "We are fawing in wuv and we will get mawied someday and *I* wespect your bwidge..."

We *were*? We *will*? You *do*? I was silent as I tried to figure out what I'd missed. I'd rarely even ever had a second date, and now I was about to be engaged?

"I won't cwoss your bwidge until you are weady," he said, looking deep into my eyes. He put his hand on my knee and that's when I started to think maybe this was what people meant when they said they were "moving too fast." I pulled his hand from my thigh and put it on his. I mean, this was all very nice, but—*what about all the other men who were going to want to be my boyfriend?*

He sighed.

"But I hope you are weady soon—because I am a nowmal man with stwong urges, and how long can you expect a man to wait?"

Now, I never think anything has anything to do with me but it was dawning on me that this required my involvement. I finally managed to squeak out, "You're so sweet, Rodney. But just so you know, there won't be any bridge crossing tonight."

He smiled. "I know that, Maywee."

He leaned into me, his nose inches from mine, and said, "So how about if tonight I just lick your bwidge a little?"

Thus ended my welationship with Wodney. ✎

Regarding Various Hardware
That Is Sent To The Cleaners
Of Such Things

I was mad with excitement when I procured an apartment in New York. It was a fourth-floor walkup slightly smaller than a handicapped bathroom stall, but it was mine, all mine, in an illegal sublet kind of way. I rented the place from a wirey older guy, Bud, who was moving to Minnesota to live with his lady friend. It was one of those classic New York situations where he was in a rent-controlled apartment and paid $400 a month for it, but was going to secretly rent it to me for $1000 a month. In the grand scheme of New York rental machinations, it was largely considered that I'd gotten a great deal.

Bud planned to leave a few things behind and when I went to his place to get the keys, he gave me a tour of the place. He began with the bookshelves.

"You could put your books here, or your videos or whatever—that's what I did," he said as he patted each shelf, offering some pointers on their use.

"Okay, now, you got your refrigerator..." and he swung the fridge door a couple of times to demonstrate how one might access its contents.

Did Bud regard me as some sort of Midwestern Nell? A wild, un-kempt child-woman with crazed eyes, unable to communicate except in grunts and gestures, staggering out of the wilderness—yet able to score a sublet in Manhattan?

I unpacked the three suitcases and arranged a few items on the bookshelves as Bud had recommended. I slept that night on the futon he'd left behind (sans instructions, mind you, so it was touch and go for a while) and I dreamed of my new exciting life and all the things I was going to do with my very own 212 area code.

Within the week the bathtub started backing up, and I'd be ankle-deep in water when I showered. I didn't want Bud to think I couldn't handle his apartment, so I set out in search of pipe unclogger stuff. The only Drano I could find at the rare Duane Reade in New York was an enormous 128 oz. jug. I lugged it to the counter and the clerk put it in a plastic *I HEART NEW YORK* bag, and I got very emotional because I, too, hearted New York.

The day was really hot, and I trudged home and shuffled up the stairs, practically dragging the enormous jug behind me. I came to my door and stared at it. There was a hole where the deadbolt lock had been. I could see straight into my apartment.

You know what I did? I put my key in the hole and twisted it in the air. I'm not kidding. My mind refused to accept the information, and I must have figured that if I just went through the motions, everything would be all right. It didn't work. The other part of the deadbolt, the "bolt" part, was still firmly in place on the inside.

I decided I was at the wrong apartment on the wrong floor, and I ran up another flight where I tried the key in the apartment directly above mine. That didn't work, so I ran up another flight of stairs and tried the apartment above that one. Now I knew full well and good where I lived, but I just wanted to be wrong. I careened back down the steps again and paused breathlessly in front of my door, staring again at the hole.

Then it came to me.

"I bet the locks are being cleaned," I thought.

Of course! The super had taken the lock and sent it to the lock cleaning service! Where it would be cleaned, and returned, and work better than ever!

Seriously. That's what went through my head. When I looked around and realized mine was the only dirty lock in the building, well, I had to face facts.

Only I wasn't sure what they were. I had never, ever in my life been almost burglarized so I was unsure what it looked like. One thing was certain—the only thing I possessed at that moment was my wallet and Drano. There was no way I was going to ditch either. New York was just a den of drain-unclogger cartels laying in wait for me to lower my guard so they could steal it.

The woman who lived across the hall from me was just coming home. Her door was painted purple with stars and moons, so I presumed her to be warm, generous and friendly. I sobbed out my story. I desperately wanted someone to explain burglary protocol to me.

She listened impassively. Her makeup was like fondant on her face and when she grimaced, it made her thick black lip liner curl up beneath her nose like a thin, debonair mustache. All she said was, "Oh. Well, I'm gonna go now."

She brushed by me into her apartment. I called out plaintively, "Okay—thank you!" I am from Minnesota, you see, and I wanted New York City to like me.

Richie came up the steps. Richie was an older fellow, an acquaintance of Bud's, who looked like an elf that had hit hard times. He lived on the sixth floor and could only take one flight at a time; then he'd rest on the steps and have a beer off the six-pack he always carried with him.

I wailed out my story as he rested on the landing. His eyebrows arched and twitched, and his mouth made Os, as if I was telling him a very curious bedtime story indeed! I took a breath, thinking he'd know exactly what to do.

"Did Bud ever tell you that I went to grade school with Vanna White?" he asked. "Man, she's doing all right for herself."

He finished his beer and crumpled the can.

"Well, anyway—good luck."

He tucked the remaining two cans of beer under his arm and started up the next flight. I did not thank him—frankly, I didn't think he'd earned it.

I slumped against the door, sobbing. When, oh when would the lock be back from the cleaners? I have a college education—though just barely—which is contained in a brain the size of a walnut with plenty of room to roam and it never, ever once occurred to me to call a locksmith.

Moments later, two workmen in the building found me propped against my door, cradling my Drano like a foundling. They used a crowbar on the door and it popped open with a crunch, and I rushed in to see for myself that my few things were still there. I had convinced myself that the wily bastards had found a way to slide everything under the door and make off with my futon, refrigerator, bookshelves—everything. I slept that night with the futon against the door, and I reluctantly called Bud the next morning. We discussed getting a new lock installed, but I am sure I heard grave disappointment in his voice. ❧

Some Things Never Change

I had no job when I came to New York, and I'd used up most of my savings in my travels.

This is what I told myself: No, you can't find a job in New York, and yes, you're destitute and demoralized—*but at least you're a loser in a cool place*. I sent out hundreds—maybe even thousands—of applications and resumes, and I just kept getting rejection letter after rejection letter. It was so maddening. I just knew that somewhere, some place, Nosal Passages Girl was getting a glowing annual review. I decided to be proactive, so I sent out my own rejection letters.

I thought that was a constructive way to spend a weekend and almost fifty dollars in stamps. Futile, yes. But it felt good. (One company actually sent my resume back to me.)

From The Desk Of....

❧ *Mary Joseph Pehl* ❧

October 23, 2000

Ms. Human Resources Person
The Thus-And-Such What-Not Company
1441 Broadway
Suite 43D
New York, NY 10018

To Whom It May Concern:

Thank you for your interest in my interest in your company. Unfortunately the position your company has does not meet my specific needs at this time.

Therefore, I am requesting the return of my resume, which will be sent to a better company with a better position. I will, however, keep my resume on file, in case another opportunity for which your company may be qualified becomes available.

Sincerely,

Mary J. Pehl

Nevertheless, it was back to temp agencies. I went to several, spent hours filling out applications and taking tests, and even they didn't want me. Apparently they didn't realize who they were dealing with: I was an *Employee of the Month!*

I confessed this pathetic plight to a friend of mine, an executive at a magazine publishing empire. He called the temp agency that his company used and got me an appointment with them. I sat in the reception area filling out yet another form, prepared to assure them I was familiar with the alphabet, and it dawned on me that in New York you have to know the right people even to temp. Someone had to pull strings so that I could *temp*! The more things change, the more they... well, you know. ❧

Can I Get Your Recipe For "Everything"? Or Is It A Family Secret?

I fell into a job as a copywriter at *Bon Appetit,* a "lifestyle" magazine devoted to all things food and entertaining. As such, I was immersed in the world of celebrity chefs, trendy restaurants, chic entertaining and recipes that called for exotic ingredients like cilantro. It may sound like it was exciting, but I was in way over my head. The only thing I really knew about food was how to get it to my mouth. My mother was equally concerned. There was silence at the other end of the line when I told her the news. "But Mary Jo…you can barely operate a microwave," she said gravely. And accurately.

I'd come by my ignorance honestly: I grew up on Tater Tots, frozen pizza and TV dinners. To me, cooking might as well have been sorcery. My entire life I thought that a "homemade cake" meant it was from a box mix; the *homemade* part was that you had dedicated yourself to adding eggs and water. And the whole extra-specialness of it was that you hadn't purchased it at a gas-station bakery.

None of this ever came up in the job interview, and so I began writing *advertorials* about fancy spatulas requiring financing and kitchen appliances that cost more than my college education, as well as proofreading exotic recipes, none of which called for Velveeta. I kept my culinary cretinism on the QT. My colleagues, after all, were people who air-kissed famous chefs. These were people who had their food not just served, but *plated*! These people knew the difference between a compote and compost, where I might have very well ordered a mixture of decayed organic material with my cheesecake.

As it was, I tested my coworkers' forbearance daily simply by being a Midwesterner. The publisher was also the home of several fashion magazines and my non-designer, plus-size attire drew tight-lipped glances. All the women wore the high-fashion, pointy-toe, spike heels that made each step percuss with a rhythmic *click-click-click* as they hoofed to and fro. Nothing gave me more pleasure than to be on the elevator as they made a run for it, and hear the change in clicking tempo as they rushed: *clickclickclickclickclickclick*. All the while I was pressing "close door." One of the managers in my department insisted on calling me Patsy, no matter how many times I corrected her. Her disdain seem to indicate that that I wasn't trying hard enough to *be* Patsy. I once mentioned that I was from Minnesota, and a workmate said with a look of confusion and pity, "Oh. That's in Maryland, right?"

All the same, the environment began to make me regard food differently. The longer I worked at the magazine, the more I became curious about this so-called "cooking" thing that people seemed to do. I was experiencing new flavors and combinations at the restaurants I sometimes got to go to; I was actually enjoying reading recipes and marveling at the sheer alchemy of it all.

But my secret shame was two-fold: not only didn't I know how to cook, I didn't even have a stove in my apartment. The one in my sublet had fritzed out years ago, and Bud never had it repaired. He'd slapped his hand on the cold burners and said I should just use a hotplate. "That's basically what a stove is," he explained. To my way of thinking, a hotplate in an dumpy efficiency apartment in New York City was tantamount to wearing three housedresses at once and going to the store in slippers and force-feeding bananas to my cats. I wanted to forestall that as long as I could. I went without.

I mentioned to my mom in one of our weekly long-distance conversations that my interest in cooking had been piqued somewhat, and I mused that it'd be nice to try it were it not for the stove situation. Dorothy asked if I'd ever considered a George Foreman Lean Mean Fat-Reducing Machine, AKA The George Foreman Grill. As I'm sure you know, it is a small, broiling appliance promoted by the former two-time heavyweight boxing champeen of the world.

She launched into an impassioned pitch for the product, positively evangelical. She herself did not own one, but her best friend did. She declared, "You know, Mary Olson does *everything* on the George Foreman Grill."

Now, I come from a family of devout consumers. They love products. They will try all sorts of products, and then buy products for their products. My mother will be like a big game hunter after coming home from a day of shopping, toting her prey in enormous crinkling bags and flushed with the tale of how she felled that particular item. I have heard her effortlessly recite complex algorithms involving ten percent off the sale price, which was already 20% off the original price, together with her senior-citizen discount and combined with an oil-change coupon that she talked the clothing store into honoring on Tax-Free Tuesday, well, "They were practically paying *me* to take it!"

My sister can quote *Consumer Reports* on any given item, and cite the month and year it was profiled. She can sum up just about anything in your home with a blurb on it.

Once my brother was in the market for a new minivan and obsessed over the purchase for weeks. I was riding along with him, his wife and three little kids when we stopped at a car dealership—on the way to my other brother's wedding, where he was going to be best man.

I hate to shop. I hate having too much stuff, and everything feels like too much stuff to me. I go to stores only when I know exactly what I need. I just *knew* this food preparation device was just another thing that people had been tricked into buying that they really didn't need, like hair styling products or eyeglasses or kidney dialysis. Still, over the course of a year, my mother brought it up every time we talked. It was always an impassioned pitch, almost word for word, to the point that I wondered if she was going door to door, asking people if they'd heard the good word of low-fat, easy to clean appliances, perhaps ending with *may I leave a pamphlet*?

And without fail, she'd conclude, "You know, Mary Olson does everything on it."

She never offered any details about what *exactly* "everything" was, and I didn't want to ask. I found the idea of anyone doing *anything* on a George Foreman Grill most disconcerting. My head was filled with images of late-night appliance debauchery, perhaps partying half-nude on the thing, dancing while raising a glass of Prohibition hooch, undulating with it in a salacious dance, rolling joints on it, or using it as an opium pipe.

And thus, because I am the Carrie Nation of products, I steadfastly resisted getting one. My mother and I were getting in strange arguments about the whole thing in a weird little power struggle. "But Mary Olson does everything on it," she'd say, sometimes pleadingly, sometimes in a "I pity you so" tone of voice, sometimes in a threatening manner.

"Really, Mom?" I'd snipe. "Cookies? Salad? Pasta? Ice cream?"

It'd become a battle of wills.

"I don't think so," I'd finish her off.

I did not want a George Foreman Grill for so many reasons. I didn't want to cook so much that I'd endanger what little status I had at *Bon Appetit*. Surely I could be fired, maybe even sued, for owning something so crude, so *declasse*, so *convenient*. Until Mary Olson became a celebrity chef or food opinion-leader, I simply could not do it.

But there it was, when I came home for the holidays and a hefty, square package was placed on my lap on Christmas Eve. My mother could hardly contain herself, she was so pleased (and a bit sauced from her yearly half glass of wine). I began to peel the wrapping paper back and my mother cried, "Yes! It's a George Foreman Grill!"

She announced to the room, "Mary Olson does *everything* on it!" She clapped for herself.

Back at work a week later, a colleague asked what I'd gotten for Christmas. I am compulsively truthful, and maybe I was a little emboldened. I mumbled the appliance that dare not speak its name and my coworker narrowed her eyes, both puzzled and suspicious.

"That's like the Tickle-Me-Elmo for Midwesterners, right?"

She might as well have thrown down the gauntlet. If Mary Olson does everything on it, then so too shall I. My recipe for George Foreman Grill Cassoulet is forthcoming. Take that, *Bon Appetit!* ❧

Postcards from China

Have managed not to starve. Subsisting on Oreos. Until lunch at an honest-to-goodness Chinese restaurant. A labyrinth of narrow alleyways brings us to a place with bags of rice, spice tins and nude fowl hanging in the window. There are only real live bona fide Chinese people eating here. I'm starving. Peter manages to convey we want to try everything. Peter will try everything. I will have the nachos.

Food just keeps coming. Plates piled high and bowls sloshing, all balanced on top of the other. Beef tendon, all sinew and muscle; pickled eggs, black and in a dark, gummy jelly; frog soup, ventricles and other various innards of said frog visible. Three waiters come to table with large tureen. One translates: "Bull penis soup!" And placed before us to the applause of neighboring tables, like the fanfare that used to accompany birthday sundae at Farrell's Ice Cream Parlor.

I blanch, apparently visibly. "For men only!" a man declares in rough English. Men who partake of it are blessed with virility. Not with me, I tell Peter. We are good friends, but not with virility benefits. China has more than a billion people, so they might be onto something. Peter tries it and rolls his eyes in gastronomic satisfaction. I hate to consider what the sandwich is for the soup n' sandwich lunch special.

If Wookiees Are Allowed To Marry, It Would Violate The Sanctity Of My Being Single

I was very upset when I discovered that Chewbacca was married. It was the mid-Nineties, I think, and some friends and I were hanging out, watching a bootleg VHS copy of the *Star Wars Christmas Special*. Oh, what a grand time we were having, laughing at the misguided, strained effort of it all.

Then Chewbacca introduced his wife.

Like *no problem*. Like *natch*.

I stared at the television in disbelief. You mean to tell me that in all the time Chewbacca and Han Solo had been work buddies, interplanetary mercenaries together, Chewie's marital status never came up? He never mentioned a *wife*?

I guess what I'm saying is that I took it kind of personally. It hit a nerve. At that moment, it summed up my whole life. Everyone—*everyone*, bar none, in the entire galaxy was in a relationship. Except me.

Even Chewbacca.

I made excuses and left the gathering, practically in tears. I walked home in the snow and obsessed, the way I'd obsessed for years about finding love and how everyone seemed to be able to do it except me. *How did people do it? How had Chewbacca and his wife met? How did she know Chewie was THE ONE? How did she manage to hold his fancy while maintaining her own identity in the relationship?*

I was awfully lonely and it was all such a mystery to me. I'd never had a boyfriend. To be sure, men liked me. *As a friend.* I was that girl that guys talked to about the girls they liked. People assured me that I was a late bloomer, but I really, really wanted to bloom before I died.

I thought romantic love was a meritocracy and hadn't I worked so hard to be lovable? Not just lovable, but a love interest, an object of someone's desire.

I strove to make the most of what I had. I'd been told I had pretty eyes and nice ankles. For a long time, I thought physical perfection won one's affections. But the more I paid attention to couples—and believe me, I was obsessed, staring at people in the mall, etc.—I began to see that that wasn't true.

So then it had to be my personality. So I worked on that. Oh, I had such a great personality. I was so nice! (For the record, I hate it when people tell me I'm nice—it makes me want to kill them.)

And then. . .

One night there was a mysterious message on my answering machine from a mysterious caller whose voice was deep and mysterious and accented.

"Mary, this is Samuel; give me a call."

No one I know calls me "Mary."

I waited a few days to return the call. Gotta play it cool, you know. I may be desperate, but I'm not *desperate*. Samuel said he'd seen my photograph in the neighborhood newspaper advertising a comedy show. He wanted to get to know me, he said, so he had looked up my number in the phone book.

"So—" he said, "You would like to meet me and I would like to meet you, and we need to meet ourselves, person to person, face to each other's face." English was not his first language. Maybe not even his second.

Then he asked, "So, Mary, what do you look for in a dating partner?"

Well, at the time, it was *someone who likes me*. Off the top of my head I spouted a laundry list of attributes: intelligent, funny, playful, curious about the world, adventurous, empathetic. . .

"But Mary! *I* am *all* those things!" Samuel gasped. And as a value-added feature, he looked like Sidney Poitier.

We agreed to meet for coffee the following week. The day before our date he called and left a message that he would not be able to make our date because he was working late.

We made another date, and that evening he called to say he couldn't make it because he hated going out in cold weather. This was *Minnesota*. He then asked if he could see me the following week—which put us even deeper into winter.

Several weeks passed. Samuel called again. "Oh, Mary," he said gravely, "Just before I was to meet you, I was rrrrrrushed to the hospital with emergency pneumonia."

I know what you're thinking. I should have just put a stop to it. But there were a couple of things going on. First, I felt it was a valuable experience to be dealing with the frustrations of this so-called "dating" that people seemed to be doing, and I assumed not ever meeting one's boyfriend in person was one of those frustrations.

Secondly, it was all kind of an anthropological sociological experiment. I was so curious to see how many times he'd cancel before he became even slightly self-conscious. He had a high threshold—it happened maybe eight times. And any fears I might have had about meeting a total stranger were allayed, because clearly Samuel was too damn lazy to harm me. Admittedly, it was kind of disappointing to be stalked by someone so half-heartedly.

It was painful but I finally had to break up with him. I had given him the best year of my life over the phone but it had run its course. I actually said, "We can't go on like this."

Samuel sighed. "Mary," he said. "I feel sorry for you—because, Mary, you will never get a chance to meet me."

I moved back to Minneapolis after a few years in New York, and guess who called? Samuel asked when we were finally going to get together.

"We need to get face to face so we can become intimate with ourselves."

I couldn't stand the thought of having known someone for so long and never having met him. Curiosity motors me.

"How 'bout right now, Samuel?"

I named a Middle Eastern restaurant and told him to be there in thirty minutes.

Don't ask me how but I just knew it was him when he strolled into the restaurant. Indeed, he resembled Sidney Poitier—in that way that all people have facial features and bodies.

I was on a date! I think. In any case, I wanted to get the conversation rolling. I asked him if he could cook. He told me assuredly and unintentionally salaciously, "Oh, yes, Mary; and some day I will cook for you and you will eat my meat!" He then remarked that his friends were curious about me, and had asked if I was pretty or not. I thought this was incredibly rude, and I felt a "boundary" snapping into place. I laid into him, launching in a diatribe and employing words like *respect* and *jerk* and *maturity* and *consideration* and *manners*.

During my passionate speech, Samuel reached over the table and grasped my nose between his finger and thumb, and tweaked it, as if playing some sort of perverse version of "Got Your Nose."

He wiggled my nose and said, "Oh, Mary, I do not judge you by what you look like."

I collected my purse and my nose, stood up and walked out. He ran after me. "Mary," he hollered, "how about giving Samuel a kiss?" His face leaned over the open car door as I was just about to drive off, and his mouth was open and tongue protruding.

I slammed the door. He pressed his face to the window.

"Mary! Pleeeeeeeze! I do not want you to think I am some sort of sexy maniac!"

And that was that. ❧

I Finally Embark Around "The Block" So That Some Day I Can Declare I've Been Around It A Time Or Two

Things really picked up when I lived in New York. Wodney was right. I was approached so often by men that I started to wonder what everyone had done before I got there. At the time, I failed to understand that if you made eye contact with a man in New York, you were basically saying, "Please, I insist you have sex with me now." (Compare this to taciturn, impassive Midwesterners for whom the old joke goes, I was in such a good mood, I almost told my wife I loved her.)

After Wodney, there was Mohammed. He worked for a car service I used to get to the airport once. (I was working my way up from cab drivers.) I could not understand him well, and he might have been flirting with me but it was hard to tell.

He said something to me several times which I did not understand.

Then he handed me a pen and said, "Your number?" And I was still saying YES! to the universe, no matter how bad its English was.

He picked me up for our date and didn't really have an action plan.

"Whatever you want to do is fine," he said.

I proposed a movie.

"Yes, if you want to."

What would he like to see?

"Whatever you want to see is fine."

That didn't seem to be panning out, so I asked him if he wanted to go to a restaurant.

"Yes, if you want to."

What kind of food did he like?

"Whatever you like is fine, Mary."

I was already exhausted.

We went to a pizza place, and when the waitress came Mohammed ordered two pizzas, a small one for himself and a large one for me. I was mad and embarrassed, and decided to call it a night. After we ate, of course. Sharing a single pizza.

Mohammed drove me home whereupon I could not get the seatbelt unfastened. He leaned over me, and brow furrowed and muttering, he fiddled with all the mechanisms. Unable to get the lock disengaged, he pulled away in frustration and his hand accidentally dragged across my chestal region.

He gave up trying to free me and stared straight ahead through the windshield. With a heavy sigh, he said, "Mary, it has been two years."

I always think I should know what people are talking about, so I nodded gravely.

"Oh."

It sounded serious, whatever it was.

He bowed his head and bit his lips.

"Yes, Mary, two years... since... I have been with a woman."

He turned to me forlornly; then, with a shrug of his shoulders, and palms upward, he made a helpless gesture to his crotch. As if to say, "I'm okay with it; I just don't know what I'm going to tell my penis."

Oh, my. But I still couldn't get out of the car. I thanked him for the delightful evening and as gracefully as I could, I flipped the seat all the way back, and scooched backwards out of the seat belt until I ended up in the back seat. I exited through the rear door and never looked back. ৯৯

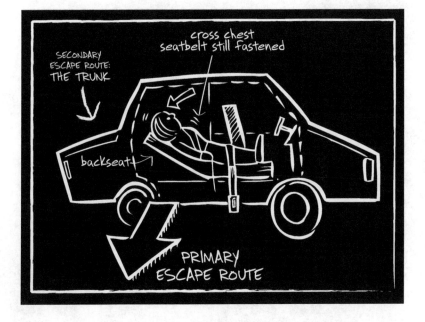

The Hard Questions

Korey was a street vendor in Greenwich Village who sold books from a table on the sidewalk. Not only was he in the literary arts, he had dreadlocks like a fountain of snakes erupting from his head and a sexy grin, and a deep, scratchy voice that made Barry White sound prepubescent. About 5'5", he always wore tight, plaid bell-bottom pants and enormous platform shoes, which, with his huge head of hair, looked like he might topple off at any moment.

Korey told me all about the retail sidewalk bookselling industry and referred to his warehouse. In hindsight I suppose that his "warehouse" was any Barnes and Noble with a lax security guard. He was Rastafarian, and, depending on when you asked him, was either from Jamaica, Ghana or Toledo. It was all so exciting. We'd

go to dance clubs and dance all night long, and I felt like I was making the scene, man.

Then one night Korey stood me up. A few weeks later I was walking home and he pulled up in an enormous SUV. Seeing me, he parked and slid down from the seat, landing safely on his platform shoes. He was happy to see me and he wanted to go out that night. Me, I was drawing more boundaries.

"I'm not going out with you—I'm really mad at you, Korey."

In his deep voice, he said, "Baby, why you say that?"

"Because we were supposed to go out last week and you blew me off."

"Baby, why you say that?"

"Because we made plans to go out on Friday and then you never showed up and you never called me to advise me of the change in plans," I said.

"Baby, why you say that?"

I was getting kind of flummoxed.

"Well, um, I guess I say that because, well, that's what happened."

Wounded, Korey swayed on his shoes slightly.

"Aw, baby, why you say that?"

Now I was getting disoriented.

"Because you blew me off, Korey."

"Now, baby. WHY you say that??" He asked sternly.

"I say that because—Okay, look, Korey, just don't ever call me again, okay?"

Korey was saddened.

"Awwwww, baby, why you sayyyyyy that?"

I didn't know whether to laugh or scream. So I said goodbye. But I admit, Korey had given me a lot to think about. Why did I say that? What makes me say the things I do? It's like I don't even recognize myself sometimes. ❧

I Thee Wed

My affianced, Ron, and I were in Target. I was armed with a scanner. I'd finally relented to "registering" for our upcoming wedding, which consists of creating a list of desired gifts from well-wishers. Why this is considered more civil than just walking up to someone and demanding a gravy boat, I'll never know. In any case, all I had to do was aim the scanner, a handheld version of what you'd find in the grocery checkout, press the trigger, and it would automatically compile a list of everything I'd be willing to accept from my humble subjects. I pointed the device at a bag of potato chips, just to see if it worked. Ron whispered conspiratorially, "Point it at my crotch! Let's see what happens!"

Long after I'd managed to be happy for Chewbacca and wish him all the best; after many years of having made my peace with singledom and enjoying my life for what it was, I was getting married.

The stranger's email had come out of the blue. All it said was, "Are you married?" No introduction, no *sincerely yours*, no nothing. It had come through my website, which I maintained for writing, acting and voice-over work in the post-*Mystery Science Theater* years.

Is this a cold call? I typed back. *Send.*

Still peeved, I immediately followed that with: *Mind introducing yourself?* Hit *send* again.

A couple of hours passed. But grudges burn deep and steady within me like a pilot light and I was intent on getting in the last word, at least one more time.

The last word became a long diatribe taking whomever to task for his or her rudeness, which morphed into indignation about the cowardice of the anonymity of the internet. Which naturally segued into a feminist manifesto with statements like, *get with it, it's the 21st century, not all women are married nor are they defined by their marital status, and guess what? I drive and vote and wear pants and just who the hell do you think you are?*

An especially emphatic *send*.

A couple of years later, we got married. Guess I showed him.

In between there were emails, in the first of which he apologized for his forthrightness. Through our exchanges over several months, I discovered he was funny and smart and practiced good punctuation. But he lived in Dallas. And to my way of thinking, regular emailing does not a "relationship" make.

We began talking on the phone now and then, and then suddenly we'd be talking for hours. Nevertheless, that still didn't constitute a relationship, and I told him that if he wanted this to be something, he must come to Minnesota to declare himself. And he'd better be prepared to meet my entire family, just in case someone had to identify him in a lineup. He did, and with grace and chivalry and good humor. And for almost a year, it was either Dallas or Minneapolis every other weekend for us. Then we moved to Austin together.

And then it was deciding to get married. It was shocking how immediately and forcefully I was *sssssucked* into the marriage-industrial complex. Even though I spent many years wanting to be in a relationship, I'd never been one of those women who fantasized and planned a wedding itself. I was sorta just thinking some Chicken-In-A-Biskit and spray cheese—maybe tap water if I could get a good deal on it, *avec* cubes *d'ice* if given plenty of lead time.

We planned to go to a judge on a Friday afternoon and have a weenie roast in my parents' backyard with just immediate family. But our circles of friends and my enormous extended family wanted to give gifts. (Some of them were just plain amazed. A dear friend of our family described a woman she worked with who was in her mid-twenties and despairing of ever finding love. The friend declared to me, "And I told her, why, do you know Mary Jo Pehl is getting married for the first time—and she's in her *mid-forties*." I'd become the Norma Rae of single gals, I guess.)

All of which brings us back to Ron and me in Target on a Tuesday night with a scanner. I can't help but wonder what the hell I'm getting into if my future husband wants me to scan his wiener area. I mean, I love him so much. More than anyone I'd ever met before, in ways I didn't know you could love someone. But I was a little frightened, too. What did it all *mean*? How do people *be* married? What if I didn't do it right? What if getting married meant that I'd never be able to pursue my dream of becoming an astronaut/ballerina/Realtor®/veterinarian? And for heaven's sake, what would we talk about every day?

These were the questions that wiggled back and forth in my brain as I scanned a jumbo bag of Ruffles. Then motor oil. CDs. Chocolate. A big screen television. A couple of mouse pads. Mini-pads. Spiral-bound notepads. I was suddenly overcome and flushed with greed. I wanted everything, and the scanner beeped and beeped and beeped.

I began to wonder if weddings weren't rather like funerals. The rituals surrounding the event keep you from thinking too much about the *great beyond*, the unknown existence after all is said and done. The Egyptians packed up their dead with riches before they were entombed so they'd have all the right stuff in the afterlife, whatever they imagined that to be. Being feted for my nuptials was the same principle. There is very little time for soul-searching if you're hell-bent on getting the pretty flower postage stamps with which to send out the invitations.

When you apply for a marriage license in Ramsey County, Minnesota, you are asked to swear that, among other things, "*neither party is mentally deficient.*" Sure, Ron had collected a doodle bug somewhere and kept it in a bowl and named it Cody Three. He'd also lately been working on his Marty Allen impersonation and spouting random "Hello, deres!" with the intensity of a Method actor. And at this moment, he stood in the shampoo aisle, hips protruded toward me, waiting expectantly. It was a loaded question, that. All I knew for sure was that there was no one else in the world whose hand I wanted to be clutching when we took that leap of faith.

Making sure no one was looking, I aimed the scanner. I hoped it wasn't like the movie *Scanners* and I'm just shooting myself in the marital relations foot by exploding his marriage tackle. I took aim and pulled the trigger. I wanted it all. ✋

A Full-On Moon

It came to pass that I would move to Austin, Texas to begin a new life with the man who would become my husband.

Every time I move, I swear I will never ever ever do it again. It must be like having a baby—you forget about the pain once it's over. My apartment was small and I thought I didn't have much, but as I organized and sorted I seemed to get nowhere. And you completely lose perspective. I had a bottle of vanilla that has made some seven moves with me over the past 25 years. I don't bake, I've never baked, I don't plan on ever baking. It just seemed like everyone should have a bottle of vanilla. What if I needed it on the long drive to Texas?

Nevertheless, I managed to sell or donate most everything and I'd gotten it all down to a mere carload of stuff. Except for the sofa, television and bike. I was stuck. They'd cost twice as much to move as they cost to purchase in the first place. Yet I wouldn't make enough by selling them to replace them once I got to Texas.

A little Googling yielded a site where people could bid on moving cargo for people. You submitted what you wanted moved and various contractors with trucks or trailers or rigs of any sort would make you an offer.

Like Earl Moon.

THANKS 4 Oppertunity to provide your damage free, transportion/ shipping. Iam a Native TEXAN 38 yrs and Home Owner Tow truck Oper/Owner 12-15 yrs Houston, TX "As a tow truck operator" I have Taken the need 4 personal/Public Safty and Responsablity above a need to speed 2 meet deadlines that FREE 4 all DOT ph/ drug screen card and safty cert. Drug free. Non drinker I have Motorcycle ramps Dolly/Pads/Tie downs. Covered/Open truck 10'25'-Boats/Hores-n-Travel trailers/RV/ATV= U ASK i hv moved it. I Transport/Tow/Trailer/Personal Commercial items =10#s 2 6000#s large bulky items.pallets/or not 2000 Dodge Pu.w topper cover top Saves us fuel cost if its FACTOR 4 U please consider our bid.10x6x6 7000lbs ENCLOSED cargo trailer.. "Value" of items w Req. Additional full value insur.avalable min $45. Payment:Cash/MO = Deposit:PAYPAL/Cash What happened 2 HONESTY and INTEGERTY in Buissness&Bidding 4 shipments I think so. Quilt/pad wrap N Plastic shrink wrap all items as need

Earl had me at "hores-n-travel…" I couldn't make heads or tails of it, but his bid was very low. He had his *safty cert* and was insured! What could possibly go wrong?

We made a deal through the site's bidding process, and Earl said that he'd be in Minnesota sometime that month. He was headed to New Hampshire to pick up a piano to deliver in Chicago, then there was the vintage motorcycle to be picked up in Southern Illinois to be brought to West Virginia, where he'd get a boat to bring to Northern Minnesota.

He'd head through the Twin Cities to pick up my stuff on his way back home to Houston. Not that he knew when that'd be exactly.

Almost midnight on a freezing Wednesday, Earl called to tell me he was on his way. Thirty minutes later, a pickup with an enclosed utility trailer pulled up to the apartment building. Earl bounded up to the door, short and wiry, a bundle of tendons with a big grin. And he talked non-stop.

He talked as he circled the couch, sizing it up like a horse trader, running his hands along the flanks, patting the back of it, everything short of cupping its testicles. He kept talking. Fast. It was like listening to an auctioneer narrate a film of his own life. He'd been an over-the-road truck driver but then found he just couldn't work for the man. He quit and decided to do his own thing. He entombed the sofa in a series of blankets and stretch wrap.

He talked about how his father had been struck and killed by a car when he'd stopped to help a stranded motorist on the interstate. "Good samaritan, my ass—dead samaritan, if you ask me." And he just kept wrapping that couch until you couldn't tell it was a couch anymore. He hoisted it on its end, and tried to strap it to the hand-truck. The straps kept slipping.

"Now that ain't gonna work, we gotta try it this way—son of a bitch—pardon my French, let's put the strap this way. . ." and he shooed away my attempts to assist. He told me that he'd discovered that the house he'd bought was next to a crack house. "Yeah, there's usually a reason why you can buy a decent house for $30,000."

All Earl did now was drive, and sleep in his truck along the way. He thought Houston had gone to hell after Hurricane Katrina victims repatriated the city. "You know why they call it The Big Easy? Because it's easy for people to rip you off there."

The sofa slipped again. "I've never seen such a bunch of thieves and cons like you got in New Orleans."

Though I hadn't asked, he offered, "I know I look small but let me tell you this, a guy messes with me, he's looking at a deadly assault."

Earl finally got the straps the way he wanted and he stepped back, satisfied. He said, more to himself than me, "See, the furniture will tell you what needs to happen—I just wasn't listening."

I sat in awe of this poet.

And Earl, all 5'6" and 140 pounds of him, got an 8-foot, 150-pound sofa down three flights of stairs. He clunked the dolly methodically, rhythmically down each step, all the while explaining why the 1920s building had been built with such wide staircases and landings.

I was exhausted after two hours of watching and listening to Earl. Earl hadn't slowed a whit. It was almost 2 a.m. and everything was finally stowed into the trailer. He asked for directions back to the freeway. I started to tell him, but then he told me so that we were both talking at the same time saying the same thing. I was walking back into the building as Earl kept talking telling me that he wasn't sure when he'd get to Austin, but he was headed straight down 35 hoping to miss the winter storms and he'd call Ron along the way. I can still see his lips moving by the light of the dashboard as he rolled up the truck window, continuing to talk even after it'd closed all the way.

He arrived in Austin as suddenly and mysteriously as he had in Minneapolis. Everything was intact, and he rebuffed the tip that Ron offered him, telling him he was on his way to Houston. That's the last we ever saw of him.

Wherever you are, Earl Moon—thank you. ✎

Now To Start Signing Documents "Mary Jo Pehl, CSD"

It's about nine a.m. one day in late March. I'm crying, sweating and swearing in a deserted bathroom stall somewhere in a remote Texas state park. I've never known such despair.

I'm trying to put a wetsuit on.

Ron, The Brand New Husband, and I are learning SCUBA, and this is the morning of our open-water dives, the final requirement toward earning our certification. In previous weeks, we'd attended classroom instruction at a scuba shop and completed training in the indoor pool.

It once seemed like such a good idea.

Up to this point, we'd been in swimsuits in the pool. I hadn't dealt with the lifeless rubber monster that was now trying to consume me, nor did I have any idea that the wetsuit would be the hardest part of the whole thing.

It's like trying to put on a leotard several sizes too small and made of tires.

At this moment, the wetsuit is barely past my knees and I am out of breath, blinded by perspiration and wondering why I ever attempt anything ever. I'm half nude, the bathroom smells, and it's very cold. All that's needed to complete this miserable scene is an empty bottle of Old Grand Dad discarded nearby, a raggamuffin child pounding at the door crying *mommy, mommy!*, and buzzards circling overhead.

I can hear the other divers milling around outside, waiting on me. One of my female classmates has gone to fetch Ron at my request. He knocks as he enters, and says with wonder and excitement, "Hey, M.J., did you see all those buzzards in the sky? Isn't that cool?" He loves all things of the natural world.

The SCUBA instruction manual and video extolled the wonders of diving, and also detailed potential hazards. Nowhere in there, however, was any warning about the possibility of one's husband beholding his wife of five months, a woman of size, trapped in a rubber contraption with some of her "size" squished out at the midway point, her arms stuck out over the remainder of the un-pulled-up part of the suit and its sleeves dangling, making her look like a forlorn, dumpy Kali. The wife has abandoned all hope and looks at her husband helplessly. I am simply not strong enough to pull the stubborn suit upward. I am literally stuck. Maybe I should have worn Spanx.

I look into Ron's eyes, tears running down my face. I eke out, "Help."

This hits home in so many ways. I was always one of those girls who was chosen last for the team, and only because somebody *had* to take the last person. I cannot bear the television show *Survivor*, because I know I'd be voted off the island on the flight to the island. Never wanting to be humiliated, I was for many years a hermit content to burrow into my couch and my books and movies. But over the years, I figured I was missing out on too many things. To hell with all that, I thought, and I started skiing and snowshoeing and taking tango lessons. I no longer cared.

After all, the axiom goes that it's good to get out of your comfort zone: you learn so much about yourself. What I learned about myself in SCUBA is that I'm buoyant—really, *really* buoyant. The greater one's BMI, the better one can float. Not to brag, but 'gifted' is probably the word to use in my case. At long last, something I excelled at!

So one must use weights attached to a belt or vest to maintain neutral buoyancy below the surface. This is so you can swim beneath the surface of the water, yet not sink to the bottom. I shan't go into graphic details about just how many pounds of weight were needed for me to achieve neutral buoyancy, but let's just say the instructor went hunting for a sofa and a spare engine block.

Still and all, I'd mastered the necessary skills in SCUBA. In fact, the instructor told me I was one of the best in the group. I'd almost allowed myself to get a little bit excited about SCUBA diving. Until now.

In this dank ladies' room in the middle of nowhere, it all comes flooding back. I'm disconsolate. I want to quit. Give up. Forget it. Everything. I want to retroactively quit everything I'd ever attempted, and *pre*-quit everything I ever thought I wanted to do.

Ron strides over to me, tall and lean, and elegantly at home in his body. He looks like an action-movie hero in his wetsuit, like he might unzip it and step out in a crisp tuxedo. He's so excited about the whole thing and can't wait to commune with turtles and fishes. I love the guy so much, and never more than when he tells me not to fret, that everyone has a hard time getting into their wetsuits. He's now braced his legs, and he yanks upward while I clutch the silver handicapped railing in the stall. My feet are momentarily raised off the floor. Think a particularly violent Mammy trussing up Scarlett if Scarlett had taken up a sport that required a ridiculous outfit.

There is thrashing, grunting and breathlessness (and not the good kind). Inch by inch, our four hands worked the stubborn material upward. Then suddenly I am in. It's up over my shoulders and I can zip it up. I am fully encased in the rubber like a helpless sausage. I waddle to the lake, like a triumphant Teletubby. I can't decide if I'm excited or relieved, but all I know is that I feel like I could do anything. Ron and I dive through the lake and I am, for a short time, weightless. All the struggle of the morning is far, far behind me.

Then I begin worrying about getting *out* of the wetsuit.

Ron? Ron, honey? ✎

Postcards from Peru

"Please, please don't get kidnapped in Peru", my mother tells me, driving me to the airport. On my way to spend a few weeks traveling the country. Assured her I would do my best, and instructed her that, should that happen, no rescue attempts were to be made until I was at least a size 10.

It's been a long time since I was anywhere that required a passport and where guidebooks recommended bringing your own toilet paper. Want to see Machu Picchu before it's gone, even though I'm assured there's a perfectly good one at some Disney World or another.

After traversing Lima for a day, head to Ica, south of Lima. Here's where the Nazca lines are, the fantastic, enormous shapes that can only be truly appreciated from the air. The sightseeing flight is about $150 and requires a release form asking for my weight. Panic. Will I be asked my weight for every monetary transaction I make in this country? Can't I just say "big-boned"?

Sightseeing plane is nothing more than a golf cart with wings. So small that my knees touch the control panel, and when the pilot fiddles with the controls his hand brushes my knees. Pilot straps notebook to his leg with a velcro strip and scribbles notes as guy on tarmac manually spins plane's propeller. Pilot continues to journal as plane gurgles down the runway. Dear Diary: This may be my last entry if large American woman lied about weight.

So this is how I am going to die. In a Barbie's Drug-Running Plane, airsick, with three complete strangers and out $150 for the pleasure. What will my family do with the three rolls of toilet paper I left in my apartment? Pilot notices I'm gagging - hands me a large green trash bag to vomit in. Appears to be 30-gallon size.

Pilot yells it'll be about forty minutes before we reach the area of the Nazca lines. I don't mean to criticize Peru, but they've known where the lines are for thousands of years and they didn't think to put the airport any closer?

"Professional Courtesy!"
(Just In Case You Are
A Joke Completist)

"Hey, I got one—"

A chill falls over the convivial table where my husband, parents and I are breaking bread at a hole-in-the-wall barbecue joint. Things had been going fine.

But now my father wants to tell a joke. He adjusts his large glasses, trifocals big as picture windows at a lake house. His pink cheeks are pinker after several novelty cocktails. The ways this could go haywire are myriad.

"Why do—?" He giggles. "No—wait…" He has to think a minute.

A huge rusted ceiling fan labors overhead and our bare elbows stick to the plastic red-and-white checkered tablecloths. An aching silence comes over us, as if Black Bart might come bursting through the saloon doors with six-shooters spraying. I'm pretty sure a clock ticks ominously in the distance.

"Honey, how does it go?" Perplexed, he turns to my mother as his fingers tap his shiny head. The punch line suddenly goes off somewhere in his brain and he starts laughing.

"Okay—when lawyers eat…" He stops short. "Hold on—"

We wait quietly. Several times over the course of the evening, my mother has waved a five-dollar bill and brashly commanded my husband, "Ron! Get some more Mike-a-ritas!"

Once again she goes for her wallet, and Ron jumps up eagerly. If ever a group of people desperately needed a margarita-flavored cocktail in a bottle, it's now.

My dad starts laughing again. "Yeah, that's it!" It has come to him.

Now, my father can pretty much do anything: He is a master craftsman and has built gorgeous, elaborate pieces of furniture, from headboards to hope chests. He can tell you what construction materials were used in any sort of house or building through the ages. He can navigate complex tax codes and earned a brokers' license in his late 60s. He can identify the sound of a 1939 Farmall Tractor from 100 paces. But this, this isn't failing memory. This is one thing he can't do after decades of trying.

"Why do—" He straightens his arms and wags his fingers before him, as if he's about to pull a rabbit out of a hat. He shifts in the hard wooden bench and moves a bottle of barbecue sauce an inch to the left, adjusts a fork ever so slightly, a stage manager at his own performance.

"Why do—why do *sharks eat their young?*" He starts roaring with laughter. He laughs his sonic-boom laugh. We remain silent. It sounds kind of familiar, this joke-like thing, but something has gone horribly awry.

Fortunately, there's always an able assistant or two at the ready, standing by to sort through the rubble, salvage what they can, and piece it all back together. My husband glances at me, then my mother.

"Um… do you mean, 'Why don't sharks eat lawyers?'"

My dad starts laughing like Ron just told the best joke ever.

"Yeah! That's it!" He is overcome with laughter.

90

For him, the setup is an annoying roadblock to the punchline, nouns and verbs but niggling details. He waves away what he clearly considers nitpicking on Ron's part. He rolls his eyes.

"Okay, okay—" He takes a deep breath, as we morons are clearly trying his patience.

"Why don't sharks eat lawyers?!"

We haven't even heard the punchline nor do we care—we've already started laughing. The *telling* of the joke has taken on a strange, beautiful life of its own, performance art at its best. Sure, it's a corny old joke, but my father has made it spectacularly his own. Maybe one of these days a joke will come out of his mouth, words all in order, delivery, set-up and punch line executed perfectly. When and if that happens, I'll be kind of sad. I'll need another Mike-a-rita indeed. ✋

Good Thing The Word Wasn't "Canine" Or This Could Take All Year

Every so often I get the urge to save the world—as long as it doesn't take up too much time and it's conveniently located. So when a neighborhood paper advertised a volunteer opportunity at a nearby elementary school for a mere thirty minutes a week, I jumped at the chance—as much as I have ever "jumped" in my life. Once a week I would sit with a first-grader as he or she read a book aloud, and help the kid practice reading skills.

This—*this* I could do. I love to read and boy, can I sit—I can outsit anyone and anything, any time anywhere, with one ass-cheek tied behind my back. And I can usually get through thirty minutes of anything without something going too horribly wrong. Usually. Never mind. Where was I?

I've loved to read since I was barely in kindergarten. I read everything I could get my hands on—my parents' faux leather-bound editions of *Reader's Digest* book compilations that lined the bookcases, all the woodworking magazines my dad got, and all the *National Geographics* he saved because they were just too beautiful to discard. And when I was in third grade, I found my older sister's copy of *Love Story*. I started—and finished—it one afternoon after school, and I called my mother at work, sobbing. *What can you say about a 25-year old-girl who died*, I wailed. Actually, since we'd been instructed to never call her at work unless we were dead, Mother had a few invective-laden things to say, which made me suspect Erich Segal had posed a rhetorical question.

Nevertheless, I was undeterred. And to this day, libraries and bookstores make me swoon, and nothing would make me happier to pile up all the books I've ever loved and roll around in them naked. (Please don't tell the Minneapolis Public Library.)

Anyway. Where was I?

So on a fine autumn day in Austin, the first day of my humanitarianism, I entered the library of the school and sat on a tiny chair waiting for Andrea. A few minutes later, a small dark-haired girl bounced toward me nonchalantly on sneakers with flashing lights in the soles, running her hands along the bookshelves. Her entrance was art unto itself, the way she casually danced and minced her way to the table where I sat. I introduced myself and asked her some questions about her life. She reported that she was five years old, she was in first grade and her teacher was Mrs. Garcia. She noted she was the youngest in her family. "My parents have four children—I'm one of them," she said, like it was a Larry King interview.

Andrea opened the book she had chosen, *Go, Dog. Go!* She bowed her face inches from the first page, upon which there was a fanciful drawing of a dog on roller skates and a single three-letter word. She pressed a tiny, grimy index finger under the first letter.

"D-d-d…" This letter was easy. She knew it and it came out confidently. At this age, kids have mostly learned the alphabet and are working on mastering the sounds and how letters pair up with other letters.

She sort of tested the next letter. I leaned in to listen to her sound it out. A breathy "O" came softly out of her mouth and I could smell the tailwinds of school lunch on her breath—who knew five-year-olds could have bad breath? This was a little harder but she got it.

The tiny fingertip slid across the page to the last letter. "Guh, guh." Very slowly, very carefully, she moved the letters around her lips, trying to shape them. I was enjoying my magnanimity up til then. But now I was getting irritated. I could feel the anxiety surging through me and my palms started sweating. For some reason, I wanted to yell, "Push! Push!" Like a midwife.

Here was this sweet, bright child, so small beside me, earnestly trying to crack the code, and I was getting kind of mad. I guess I was surprised at how stupid a child could be. I'm not proud of that, I'm just telling it like it is. I wanted to yell, "Look at the picture, fer cryin' out loud! *Could it be more obvious?*" Which, of course, would be one of those rhetorical questions.

I was thisssss close to just snatching the book away from her and huffing, "Oh, just let *me* do it."

And I was thisssss close to being a "Great Santini." I was just a "This Boy's Life" memoir waiting to happen. It took my entire wherewithal to just breathe, and get out of the way and let it happen.

She suddenly cried out "Dog!" She smiled triumphantly, and sat back in her chair with a sort of relief. And so it went for the next twenty minutes. When the half-hour was finished, we were not even a third of the way through the book. I was exhausted. It was hard going, this saving of the world, one word and thirty minutes at a time. Honestly, I'd have an easier time in the Peace Corps.

I fought the urge to tell her that someday it would all make sense, the maddening letters would come together to form exquisite sonnets, magnificent stories about white whales, and banal Twitter entries. And through the next several months, we managed to get through *Clifford The Big Red Dog*. We never did get to *Love Story*.

I hope Andrea grows to love reading as much as I did. But seriously, that girl has got to get her act together. ✤

A Love Forbidden

Along time ago, I once loved a very special cheese. You are no doubt shocked, as our love is frowned upon by the draconian social conventions of our time, and given the strict caste system of the food chain, I am forbidden to wed any nutriment beneath me. But I loved cheese more than any dairy product I have ever known before; nay, more than any item on nay, more than any item on the little blue dish on the upper-right side of the USDA's MyPlate graphic! There! I don't care if the whole world knows it!

Let me start at the beginning. I had gone out for a late-night dinner with the man whom I was psychically commanding to be my boyfriend. We ordered a cheeseburger to split, and the waitress wanted to know what kind of cheese we wanted. As far as I was concerned this was none of her business and I rebuffed her meddling.

Nonetheless, Steve urged me to try the pepperjack. I was apprehensive—I am always nervous around new cheeses, but I relented. The waitress left, seemingly satisfied with this information, and Steve assured me that she would not use it for malicious or seditious purposes. We continued our conversation, and I continued to telepathically will him to be my boyfriend.

The hamburger arrived and Steve cut it in half. I was still able to sustain my silent mind control of him, and I couldn't help but notice that the the manner in which he offered me the ketchup seemed overtly romantic, if not downright erotic, though some might use the word "perfunctory". Be that as it may. I was apprehensive but I steadied myself and took a dainty bite. It was that moment that I fell madly, wildly in love. Here I suppose you are cheering Steve's and my nuptials—but it was not he with whom in love fell I.

"Steve? Steve *who*?" I asked myself—facetiously, of course, for I knew Steve who, as he was sitting right beside me and I use hyperbole to illustrate my abrupt indifference to Steve. You see, before that moment I had not known cheese. And while Steve obliviously salted his french fries I instantaneously released him from my psychic grip, and pepperjack and I made hushed plans to elope that very morrow.

The next morning I set about happily packing my trousseau. Pepperjack and I had planned a private ceremony on a secluded beach in the Bahamas and the bus left in just a couple of hours. The doorbell rang. Surely this was my beloved cheese come to whisk me away to the Greyhound station to begin our new lives together!

I flung the door open. It was my father wearing a t-shirt emblazoned with the delightful aphorism *You'll Get My Gun When You Pry It Out of My Cold, Dead Hands* and a jaunty cap bearing the epigram *When Guns Are Outlawed Only Outlaws Will Have Guns*. I always delighted in Daddy's witticisms, and then I saw a shotgun in his hands.

He burst through the door. "Where's the cheese?!" he yelled. "Where's that no-good son of a—?!" My heart hammered with fear. How had Daddy learned about Pepperjack and me? Had Steve seen our clandestine canoodling and then alerted my father? He *knew* Daddy was virulently lactose-intolerant! This could only be Steve's vicious retaliation for me having ceased my psychic control of him.

"Daddy," I said, "Daddy, calm down." At that very moment, my pepperjack came bounding up the sidewalk clutching a single red rose. Father whirled around.

"Daddy, no!" I cried. It was too late. A shot rang out and my pepperjack crumbled to the ground in a heap, bits of curds splattered on the steps. The rose fell from his grasp. I flung myself over the lifeless wedge and wept. My beloved dairy product died there, on the threshold of our lives together.

People have tried to comfort me by saying things like, "There are other cheeses, dear," or "Better this than having to watch him die a long, painful death from something like mold." Even my best friend said, "He's in a better place now." But I cannot imagine that laying in a landfill somewhere amidst disposable diapers, frozen pizza boxes and banana peels is "a better place."

So you see—love does not conquer all. For Pepperjack and I have tried. ❧

The Worm!
Or Whatever It Is, I'm Against It

I can see the downside to pretty much everything. Wait, hang on. No, *everything*.

An opportunity came along for which I'd been sorta, kinda excited. I had an opportunity to interview and write about Father Jerry Hogan, a Catholic priest who travels with Ringling Bros. and Barnum & Bailey circus. This just seemed so fascinating, so fun. It was right up my alley: I, who'd been raised Catholic and was myself in this business called show!

But whenever anything good happens, I start thinking, "What's the catch?" Somewhere there is always a shoe waiting to drop. Unbridled enthusiasm has never been part of my constitution. When subjected to the age-old litmus test, *Do you see the glass as half empty or half full?* I will respond with outrage, *You got a glass? How did you get a glass?*

I'd heard about the priest and made many calls and written many emails. After a couple of months, Ringling Bros. gave their permission and the priest agreed to the interview. But the closest the circus would be for a long while was Cleveland. I enlisted my friend Tim and his camera to come for company and some laughs for the long drive across the Midwest. We left Minneapolis in high spirits.

Then somewhere in Wisconsin I saw a bull urinating. The creature was off in a pasture, but even from that distance one could see the powerful, coursing stream. It was astonishing, really. The bull was peeing like a racehorse and what's more, he just seemed so *casual* about the whole thing.

I poked Tim from the driver's seat to see it, but by the time he located the animal on the horizon, the bull had wrapped things up. Tim seemed irritated. "Why didn't you point it out sooner?"

I was defensive. "It happened so fast!"

We were only in Wisconsin and things were getting testy.

We were silent for awhile… then we tried to make each other laugh. We began mocking everything. *Everything.* We taunted the misspelled homemade signs for cheese and eggs and *pupies 4 sail*; we jeered people's political sensibilities evidenced by their bumper stickers; and we even ridiculed trees. Trees. Look, I'm not proud of it, I'm just telling it like it is.

It got almost feverish in that small car, each of us trying to outdo the other in our scorn for everything. By the time we got to a Super 8 just outside Cleveland, I was burned out from fourteen hours of driving and simply exhausted from my snarkiness. I mean, really—what had trees ever done to me? (Give me a second, I'll think of something.) No matter—whatever excitement and curiosity I might have about interviewing Father Circus had dried up, and a grimness overtook me. This was just another stupid idea which wouldn't amount to a damn thing. I crawled into bed and pulled the bedspread over my head.

The next morning we went to the arena as the circus readied for the night's performance. For hours, we trailed Father Hogan through the bowels of the arena. It blew my mind. It was crazy, elephants being walked by us within arm's length, cranky lions pacing in their cages while their handlers played cards at a table nearby, and clowns in partial makeup talking on their cellphones.

It was all I could do to match the priest's quick pace and take notes as he talked nonstop. He met with some young acrobats about their First Communions, and discussed a baby's baptism with the lion tamer and his wife. A couple walked by and Fr. Hogan nudged me, whispering, "They get shot out of the cannon together—they're having marital difficulties." Oh, how I love stuff like that—and maybe this would be okay after all.

Tim and I were invited to stay for the show, and after saying goodbye to Rev. Circus, we found our seats. I started fretting: I obsessed over all the questions I should have asked and I perseverated on all the stupid stuff I'd probably said. I started to panic about how I was going to write the story and just who the hell did I think I was, anyway? The the lights went down and from out of nowhere I got really sad because I hadn't become a trapeze artist.

The spotlights criss-crossed and the pageant began: the lion tamer put the lions and tigers through their paces; the trapeze artists swung to and fro, seemingly miles off the ground; and tightrope walkers' tiny feet walked the rope that seemed the width of twine. Oh, the spectacle!

But all I could think was, "Any one of them could die at any minute."

Then the spotlights focused on the center ring, where a group of boys stood dressed in a costume designer's version of urban streetwear. Rap music started blaring and the boys pulled out a bunch of jump ropes. They started jumping rope. Serious, double-dutch, logistically impossible jump-roping. Bounding back and forth through the ropes they somersaulted, did elaborate dance steps, bounced basketballs, balanced atop one another's shoulders, all fast and furious and dizzying.

All I could think of was leaving early to beat the rush out of the parking lot.

Out of the corner of my eye I could see a kid sitting behind me. He was maybe seven or eight, and he was absolutely enraptured. He was leaning so far forward in his seat that his "Oh, wows!" ruffled my hair. Suddenly a young man in the center ring collapsed dramatically to his stomach and began flopping over the flying ropes. The kid behind me began to holler, "He's doing the worm! He's *doing the worm!*"

The worm, as I'm sure you know, being the breakdancing fool that you no doubt are, is sometimes called a dolphin. It is a dance move in which the person lays on the ground and makes a rippling, shuddering motion from head to toe.

The kid knew this. He shrieked down the aisle, "Mom! Mom! He's doing the worm!" He couldn't bear it; his small body couldn't contain it. He was desperate to impart the magnitude of this. "Ohhh, my god, Mom! THE WORM!"

I was beholding someone beholding a miracle. I imagined the boy wouldn't be able to sleep that night, playing the spectacle over and over in his mind (well, between that and all the cotton candy). I wondered if he might try to describe what he'd seen and maybe some of his friends would say so what? Or maybe he'd practice his worm and dream about joining the circus now that there were breakdancing opportunities with the Big Top.

The lights came up after the big closing number and the confetti fluttered to rest among the sawdust. We stood up, and Tim and I watched the kid take his mother's hand to leave. He said with quiet conviction, "You know, Mom, this really *is* the greatest show on earth."

Whatever it is that makes me wary of getting too carried away about anything, whether it's my nature, my upbringing or just the years that maybe erode the unevenness of excitement, I think that kid knew something I didn't. I can recall his sweet, freckled face looking up to his mother's and being so sure about something. I try to remember that on any given day, someone, somewhere, is doing the worm, he's *doing the worm!* ✌

Postcards from Peru

Bus to Cuzco, bus from there to Machu Picchu. Bus on winding mountain roads so narrow you can't see them when you look down out the window. You just see dropoff. No, THIS is how I will die. Carsick, tired, shorts still up my butt, I don't even care. In fact, I brighten at the possibility.

Now must hike from the foothills to MP. Trip several times lumbering up path, certain I will have to be airlifted by a team of rescue workers who will mutter "lard ass" in Spanish under their breaths, and I should have learned Spanish so I know what to listen for and I'm irritated with Peru, it thinks it's so great C'mon GET IT TOGETHER PERU and I have no goddamn idea why I'm here and I am mostly so damn sick of me. Last step, I'm done, no mas — and suddenly Machu Picchu spreads before me, a dream, beautiful, haunting, and I'm overcome, bawling. Probably the thin air. Or the shorts.

The Moment

My sister said, "Do you think my life was ruined?"

Long pause.

"I've been happy since then," she said.

We were floating in inner tubes on a river somewhere in Minnesota. Nearby her three boys and another of my nephews played, rambunctious in the water, each seeming to have seven legs and twelve arms. They hollered and brawled in their play, and in their skinny youth, their limbs seemed to clank like errant machinery. My sister and I floated, something I rarely allowed myself to do, just float. I was home from New York for one week that summer, and I had decided fiercely and steadfastly that I was going to be *in!the!moment!dammit!*

Jeanne's question drifted toward me. Dark-haired, brown-eyed and slim, she is the photo-negative of me, blonde, blue-eyed, fleshy. She'll end up tanning effortlessly on the water, the way she managed to do most everything. I had slathered myself in 60 SPF. With my pink-white skin, I live in fear of getting sunburned, and I briefly considered that at the very least, perhaps I ought to have worn a snowmobile suit, maybe a sleeping bag, out on the river.

We were talking about happiness: what it meant, who we'd decided deserved it, who we deigned did not. She asked again. "Do you think my life was ruined when Timothy died?" Timothy was her youngest child and he was not quite a year old when he died in the kind of accidental drowning that might warrant a Dear Abby cautionary tale, *please, Abby, tell your readers.*

I idolized my older sister when we were growing up. She was so glamorous. She looked like Ali MacGraw, and she sewed her own halter-tops and bell bottoms and macramed her own belts. My family lived on a small lake, a sort of glorified pond, and our summers were spent in the water. I spent a lot of time on the shore, self-conscious in a bathing suit and fearful of the sun. My father had made a wooden bench on the shoreline, and I'd watch the neighborhood boys who would come over to swim with my teenage older sisters. They'd holler and push each other off the raft for my sisters' benefit. The only time boys ever talked to me was to ask about my sisters.

She hooked her foot on my inner-tube so we wouldn't float apart. The boys splashed and crashed and yelled insults and rules for their games. Sometimes I work so damn hard at being in the moment that it feels like clenching a fistful of water.

"Well?"

Her inner tube twisted away from me in the greenish-blue current, and I could see only the back of her dark head and her freckled shoulders over the plump inner tube.

I was a little afraid to admit that I too had been happy since then. She was still my big sister, I wasn't so sure she wouldn't clock me for my audacity. The current pushed us close to the shore, and we tugged on tree branches bowing over the shoreline to propel ourselves out to deeper water. It has been going on twenty years, and it feels as though our family has held its collective breath, wondering if Timothy's death was a talisman against anything bad ever happening to us again, or merely the beginning of a slippery slope.

Maybe I once thought that our lives would never be the same, though I don't really know what "the same" would have been. Over the years Jeanne mentioned a detail here and there about the incident, quietly, casually, never looking at me, while she was doing dishes or tying a child's shoe. She told me a particular memory to which I said, "I wish I could take that from you." She said, expertly carving up a cantaloupe, "If you took that from me, then what would I have?" She said it to the cantaloupe.

Our asses scraped against the rocks on the bottom of the river as we neared shore. The day was dwindling and the sun smirked behind the trees, and we started laughing about our family legacy of big butts. "I've been happy since then," she said. The water twisted her away from me again and she watched the boys' horseplay.

"For everything that's happened, I don't believe the world is a terrible place."

The boys came crashing around us and pushed us to shore as we paddled, greatly exaggerating their labor with enormous huffs and puffs and pretend exhaustion. We packed up the sandwiches and sunscreen and towels and headed home after a day on a river somewhere. We have always teased Jeanne that she knows everything, and I think she just might. ✌

Some Thoughts On The Talkies

When I was a teenager, I was very much in demand as a babysitter in my neighborhood. Hardly a Saturday night went by that I wasn't being paid fifty cents an hour to ignore children and eat potato chips and ice cream. Cable did not yet exist, and network television ran old movies well into the wee hours.

After the kids were in bed (no more than ten minutes after their parents' departure, I assure you), I usually became unnerved by the silence of the big split-level homes that populated the area. I was impressionable: I had seen *When a Stranger Calls* and I believed that the calls were coming from inside the house.

While I got that *The Creature from the Black Lagoon* and *Frankenstein Meets the Wolf Man* were intended as fright movies, I was a

leeeeetle more confident that an anthropomorphic amphibious creature *probably* would not break into the house and attack me. I could
scoff at lupine men (except the impossibly woolly, large elderly man
next door who washed his car every other day in the summer wearing only Speedos—srsly!). It was the very sound of dialogue, people
interacting on the small screen, that kept me company in the late-
night silence.

The thing is, I didn't really get that they were bad. I knew they
were fantastical, sure, but I kind of took them at face value. I think
I thought, oh, I guess people buy this kind of stuff. And since I was
always trying to fit in and figure out what it was I was supposed to be
doing, I went along.

But as I got older, I really began to question things. As with all art,
film can provoke, stimulate, challenge us as individuals and as a soci-
ety. Our lives are reflected back to us, and films dare to ask the tough
questions about ourselves.

Like…

Can women really have it all?

Most certainly. I refer you to *The Sound of Music*, which illus-
trates that you can be a nun and marry a foxy, rich, decorated cap-
tain in the Austrian Navy—and get an instant family without doing
the icky stuff you have to do to have babies! That couldn't be *more*
having it all.

I was a chubby little Catholic kindergartner when I saw my first
movie in an actual movie theater and not on *The Wonderful World of
Disney*. Since that first magical encounter, I suppose I have seen *TSoM*
at least thirty times, what with owning the collector's edition DVD,
attending the sing-along at the Uptown Theater in Minneapolis a
few years ago, and the numerous television broadcasts (which, with
the myriad commercials adding to its already long running time,
makes it just a few minutes short of the Third Reich itself). I discover
something new with every viewing… like more questions. For instance, upon roughly the millionth viewing, I suddenly wondered…

A. Why does Austria, a landlocked country, have a Navy?

    1. And more importantly, *how* does Austria have a Navy?

        a. Not to be nosy, but where are they keeping their ships? At a Public Storage somewhere off the interstate?

            i. Is it really practical?

                1. And should I become a domestic affairs advisor to countries to troubleshoot such things?

Films help us understand the human—and non-human—condition. I'm sure you've wondered, as have I…

Do other people and sentient creatures have problems, just like me?

Movies teach us that, yes, they sure do! Not only do I adore the motion pictures, they are salve when I am going through tough times. Like one particular period in my twenties—and by that I mean my entire twenties. I couldn't keep a job, I was lonely and broke, and had no idea what I was doing with life.

I discovered that *Gandhi*, *E. T.*, and the kids in *St. Elmo's Fire* had problems too. There was Mahatma Gandhi, spearheading India's peaceful resistance movement against its colonial rulers. But it was nothing like what the kids in *St. Elmo's Fire* had to face. They were college graduates facing a time of uncertainty and discovering themselves. I'll have to stop here—I start crying just to think of it.

Mary Jo, why didn't Nick and Honey just stay home?

We may never know. But anyone who thinks it's a good idea to go to your boss's house when you're tipsy, your wife is getting there, and his wife is an over-the-top battle ax and they don't even break out the Chicken In A Biscuit, well, they get what they deserve.

Why don't zombies just eat each other?

It's obvious that zombies have few, if any, laws or mores governing their social interactions, so one can surmise that the cultural taboo against cannibalism does not apply. Don't try to tell me that zombies need *fresh* meat. The undead routinely demonstrate indiscriminate tastes: look at some of the live flesh they'll eat. And how about the zombie gal who eats the bug off the tree in *Night of the Living Dead*. Lord only knows where that bug has been!

It is generally understood that a zombie is a human corpse that has been brought back to a sort of life. The dead can be reanimated by various methods: sometimes witchcraft is used. In other instances, zombies get their second life from biotoxins, chemicals or radiation gone awry, as in *Night of the Living Dead* and *I Am Legend*. In *Pet Sematary*, the dead are reactivated after being interred in an ancient burial ground. (Important take-away from *Pet Sematary*: don't reanimate a toddler—toddler zombies are particularly vengeful.)

Zombies can no longer speak, nor do they recall their former humanness. They usually lumber about slowly and stiffly, working against the *rigor mortis* that has begun to set in before they were reanimated. (Surely it must be terrifying to see such a beast shambling toward you, but their sluggishness must also tax any victim's patience.) And although they may be persistent and unflappable, qualities that would serve them well in just about any job, zombies are also unreasonable, impervious to reason and cold to one's beseeching. They will invariably destroy your car and/or your house and/or other personal belongings. They are indifferent to personal hygiene. They search for food in groups—and we all know how annoying cliques are.

And the food zombies ruthlessly seek is human flesh. That's *you* and *me*, friend. Story upon story shows zombies tucking into humans like so much potato salad at a church picnic. What's more, they help themselves to the flesh of the living *without ever asking permission*. This is where their heretofore annoying behavior crosses the line.

Some zombie films posit that they must eat brains exclusively, because it eases the pain of unlife. They should take a page from the playbook of the living: Liquor. Booze. Alcohol.

Which all leads us to another question we must seriously consider - could it be that zombies are assholes?

And speaking of eating, would Jill Kinmont ever be able to eat potato chips again?

The Other Side of the Mountain is the story of Jill Kinmont, an Olympic skiing hopeful whose dreams are dashed in an accident on the slopes that leaves her paralyzed from the neck down. The only scene I remember with crystal clarity, even after seeing it in the mid-seventies, is when she attempts to pick up and eat a single potato chip after months of arduous physical therapy. She does this to demonstrate to her jerky, shallow fiance how far she's come in her rehabilitation. The fact that she might never again eat a potato chip was the most heartbreaking part of the movie for me. I couldn't think of anything else during the rest of the film. What about the potato chips and other snack foods? Why this film is not included in the pantheon of great food movies like *Babette's Feast, Big Night,* or *Eat Drink Man Woman* is beyond me. On the other hand—potato chips? You could do worse. Maybe she could go into babysitting. ❧

Postcards from Peru

Days later, Puerto Maldonado, at the edge of the Amazon basin. A bus takes a group of us up the Tambopata River to a remote lodge deep in the jungle. We get up early for a hike in the rain forest. Hate getting up early. I can take or leave nature, but I'm afraid everyone will talk about me if I'm not there.

Enormous cicada towers, almost a foot high, straight upward, virtual insect high-rise condominiums. Everywhere on our path. Guide points them out and I step on one as I try to get out of his way. Stern older German woman points it out: "You know", she said, "If you were Buddhist, you are not supposed to kill any living thing." Hot, tired, shorts riding up (I should have hired an assistant to trail me and pull them down as I stride) I snap. "Ah, but I'm an American - we kill everything."

From Hell It Came

The guy leaned across the table and pushed a DVD box toward me. It was just after midnight and my colleagues and I had just concluded the second show of a Cinematic Titanic double-feature. Now came the time we'd meet the people who'd come to the show, all those *Mystery Science Theater 3000* fans who were now coming to see the live version, Cinematic Titanic.

He wore a faded, ill-fitting *Dr. Who* t-shirt and dated, slightly askew eyeglasses. In his arms he cradled all manner of memorabilia: a *Mystery Science Theater* movie poster, carefully labeled VHS tapes, a pristine t-shirt and some Cinematic Titanic merchandise. He parked himself in front of the table.

"I have to ask you—" he adjusted his glasses and rocked on his feet.

"In episode 821, *Time Chasers*, right? Pearl invites Mike over for coffee, but—"

"Cocoa," I corrected him.

"—Mike comes over for hot cocoa but you're the evil nemesis—"

He was referring to the characters Mike Nelson and I played on *Mystery Science Theater*. He barely acknowledged the DVD that I signed and pushed back across the table to him.

"It just didn't make any sense!" he exclaimed, his shoulders dropping helplessly. "Why would Pearl suddenly be *so nice?*"

It's hard to explain, the devotion that *Mystery Science Theater 3000* engendered. It was a low-budget television show produced in the Twin Cities from the late 1980s to late 90s. You might recognize it by the bad, cheap movies superimposed with silhouettes of the characters, who mocked the absurd plots, amateur acting, cheap production values and other hilarious flaws of the films.

The premise was that Joel Hodgson, the show's creator, had been entrapped upon a satellite in space as part of an evil experiment by some mad scientists, played by Trace Beaulieu and Frank Conniff. Joel had built two robots, Crow T. Robot and Tom Servo, fashioned out of a lacrosse mask and a gumball machine, respectively, among other objects. They were first puppeteered by Trace and Kevin Murphy, and then Bill Corbett took over for Trace, after Mike Nelson took over for Joel.

These matters did not concern the fellow standing there. He didn't take issue with the fact that my character drove a VW mini-bus in *outer space*; nor did he express any skepticism about the henchmen at one point, a talking ape and a guy who carried his brain around in a pan. In that particular scene, Mike floats over from the satellite—in space, sans any sort of protective suit – to the VW, where I as Pearl am sitting in the door, wearing only a sweater—*in the vacuum of space*. These things, no problem.

Why is Pearl suddenly so nice?

MST3K, as it came to be known, had its devotees who were, well, devoted. "*Obsessed*" might not be too strong a word.

I mean, I know this guy. He's watched the episodes over and over again, he can cite them by number, and he's dissected them with like-minded folks through chatrooms, discussion boards, meetups and conventions. For a long time, I didn't get it. On account of my chronic dull-wittedness, it took some time to make the connection that the wonderful job I reported to five days a week, Monday through Friday, was actually beamed out over the airwaves to actual living, breathing, viewing *other people*. Enough other people to constitute a cult following.

We'd get fan letters of the handwritten, post-office delivered variety. Sometimes they included toenail clippings. (Some people assumed we shared their outrageous sense of humor, right down to the little toe.) Fans took tours of the humble office and studio in a generic suburb in a generic office park. You'd get gentle lectures on the laws of physics: there's no way a vacuum tube could reach from earth to a satellite to send the movies and still be effective. People built their own Crows and Servos. Some dressed up like characters from the show. It all started to dawn on me when I met a guy at a convention who was dressed like Pearl Forrester. The likeness was astonishing, downright startling: right down to the neon green pantsuit, frightening makeup, and lots and lots of padding in all the right places.

So… quick question: *Who* are *you people?!*

I simply have no frame of reference. I'd never even seen *Mystery Science Theater* before I started as a writer, as I did not own a television for years. For me the only thing roughly analogous was *L.A. Law*. I was a diehard fan of *L.A. Law* for several years when it began airing in the Eighties. Never missed a show; could tell you the backstory of every character (whether you wanted to know or not), I could cite each character's connection to every other character, what actors played whom and what their IMDb background was—*before* IMDb even existed.

But I never attended *L.A. Law* conventions dressed like Arnie Becker. Never did I challenge any inconsistencies or the general universe of the show. (Perhaps they escaped me, I who am lost two minutes into *Murder, She Wrote*.) I simply loved the show and didn't challenge it.

Maybe it's the communal nature of it. *MST3K* rallied that desire to talk back to the screen and challenge what was being presented. People love to watch movies with other people. I wonder too if the very nature of the big screen, imposing and canopy-like, presents a certain authority by the sheer scope of its presentation. I mean, I thought *The Sound of Music* was a documentary, for cryin' out loud! It was on the big screen, it was loud, it was all-encompassing, the medium itself exuded authority.

But there was *MST3K*—on the small screen, letting out all the air of the pompousness and self-importance and attempts at grandiosity. And people talked back—something they've probably done since movies, nay, probably any art form was invented.

Who knows? All I know is that I'm a former—and possibly future—temp who is being asked for an autograph right now. The guy sat through two really bad movies in a crowded theater in uncomfortable chairs and has waited in line to meet the cast to boot. I'm a nerd/geek/hermit myself, on the shy side when left to my own devices, so it's strange for me. And there was a learning curve. No etiquette book in the world prepares you for, say, the *MST3K* convention at which a young man came through an autograph line. When he got to me, he pulled back and clutched his autograph book close to his chest. He said tersely, "I'm sure *you're* fine, but I *hate* Pearl Forrester." As if I might wrestle the book from him and force my signature upon him.

Or being declared the Yoko Ono of *Mystery Science Theater 3000*. Someone in a chatroom or discussion board angrily pointed out that the show was cancelled after I joined it. Seven years *after* I joined it. After several cast changes. And this was on a discussion board taking place ten years after the show was cancelled.

Yeah... maybe "obsessed" might be the word.

There was the time I was living in New York, a few years after

MST3K had gone off the air. I went to the movies one afternoon, and in a mostly empty theater a couple was sitting a few rows in front of me. They kept chatting loudly during the movie—something that, believe it or not, drives me absolutely batty. In front of them sat a woman, utterly irritated, who turned around and told them to kindly shut up. She hissed, "This isn't *Mystery Science Theater*, you know!"

I learned not to take it too seriously. After all, it was just this really great job where we got to sit on fat comfy couches watching wonderfully awfully bad movies with some of the smartest, funniest, terrificest people I'd ever known. (Although we never got to do *From Hell It Came*, one of my all-time favorites about a vengeful tree. What's not to love?) My job just happened to get seen and appreciated by a lot of people. I got to meet many wonderful aficionados who were fearless in their passion and devotion to something they absolutely adored – and who had a sense of humor about themselves.

So I tease the young man. "What? Pearl is driving around in space in a Volkswagen bus and *that* you'll buy?"

And maybe one of these days I just may drag out the sewing machine and whip up a Grace Van Owen costume. Who knows when there will be an *L.A. Law* convention 'round these parts? ✎

THANKS A MILLION

Thanks to:

The smart, steadfast, stalwart Tom Dupree, who kindly
guided me through this process and edited the manuscript.

The amazing Steve Schirra who brought it
to life with the design.

And...

Alonso Duralde
Liz Lent
Andrew Putz
Meleah Maynard
Joe Barlow
Trace Beaulieu
Joel Hoekstra
Barrie Jean Borich
KLW
Dorothy & Jerry

Inspected by _____

FOR A TRANSCRIPT OF THIS BOOK,
GO TO MJPEHL.COM

About the Author

 **Mary Jo Pehl** is a writer/performer/producer with *Cinematic Titanic,* the live version of the Peabody Award-winning and Emmy-nominated TV series *Mystery Science Theater 3000,* for which she was a writer and on-air actor in the recurring role of "Pearl Forrester." For these two projects, she has bravely withstood hundreds of the worst movies ever made. The experience hasn't killed her, only made her stronger.

Mary Jo has worn out packs of pencils for *Austin Monthly, Austin Chronicle, Minnesota Monthly, Minneapolis StarTribune, Catholic Digest, Salon.com,* PBS and more. Her work is featured in several anthologies, including *Life's A Stitch: The Best of Contemporary Women's Humor* and *Travelers' Tales: The Thong Also Rises.* Her commentaries have aired on NPR's *All Things Considered* and *Weekend America,* and *The Savvy Traveler* on Public Radio International.

As a standup comedian, Mary Jo has appeared on Comedy Central and A&E, and in stage productions in New York and Los Angeles. She has also contributed to *RiffTrax.* A native of Minnesota, Mary Jo lives in Austin, Texas with Ron and Seymour.